stitch style

Mittens

20 Fashion
Knit and
Crochet
Patterns

COLLINS & BROWN

Introduction

From trendy teenage girls to thirty-something professionals, everyone is knitting and hand-stitching these days. **Stitch Style Mittens** is a collection of contemporary and urban projects that'll keep you constantly inspired and motivated. From chunky knits for chilly days to lacy arm candy that will add a touch of fun to any outfit, there's a style here for every season and occasion. Best of all, the projects are portable, so you're free to knit anywhere you go. **Stitch Style** is a strand of books designed for fashion-loving handcrafters, which features an array of memorable styles inspired by everything from the catwalk to street fashion. All the designs have been created by talented knitters and trendsetters with a penchant for craft.

Kim chstyle

ens

First published in the UK in 2007 by
Collins & Brown
10 Southcombe Street
London
W14 0RA

An imprint of Anova Books Company Ltd

Commissioning Editor: Michelle Lo
Design Manager: Gemma Wilson
Photographer: Mario Guarino
Designer: Clare Barber
Editor: Marie Clayton
Assistant Editor: Katie Hudson
Illustrator: Kang Chen
Senior Production Controller: Morna McPherson

ISBN 978-1-84340-415-6

A CIP catalogue for this book is available from
the British Library.

9 8 7 6 5 4 3 2 1

Reproduction by Spectrum Colour Ltd, UK
Printed and bound by SNP Leefung, China

This book can be ordered direct from the
publisher. Contact the marketing department, but
try your bookshop first.

www.anovabooks.com

Contents

Spot-On Mittens

Made with an array of colourful polkadots, these toasty hand-warmers really hit the spot. The yarn carried across the back of the work adds a double thickness. Designed by Judy Furlong.

YARN

Jamieson & Smith *2-ply Jumper Weight* (100% wool), approx. 25g/115m per ball

- 5 balls of Cream 1A **(MC)**
- 5 balls of Deep Blue FC37 **(A)**
- 5 balls of Pink FC6 **(B)**
- 5 balls of Pale Blue FC15 **(C)**
- 5 balls of Deep Pink 72 **(D)**

NEEDLES

Pair of 3.25mm (US 3) knitting needles
Pair of 2.75mm (US 2) knitting needles
Two stitch markers
Yarn needle

TENSION

28 sts and 36 rows = 10cm (4in) square measured over St st using 3.25mm (US 3) needles.

TO FIT

One size

SKILL LEVEL

Intermediate

SPECIAL ABBREVIATIONS

See page 95 for information on double cast off.

PATTERN

Row 1: K24 in MC, PM, m1 in MC, k2 in MC, m1 in MC, PM, knit to end in MC.

Row 2: P1 in MC, *p2 in MC, 2 in A, 2 in MC; rep from * three more times, k2 in MC, 2 in A, 1 in MC, SM, p1 in MC, 2 in A, 1 in MC, slip next marker, p1 in MC, 2 in A, 2 in MC, *2 in MC, 2 in A, 2 in MC; rep from * twice more, p1 in MC.

Row 3: K1 in MC, *k1 in MC, 4 in A, 1 in MC; rep from * two more times, k1 in MC, 4 in A, SM, m1 in MC, k4 in A, m1 in MC, SM, k4 in A, 1 in MC, *1 in MC, 4 in A, 1 in MC; rep from * three more times, k1 in MC.

Row 4: P1 in MC, *p1 in MC, 4 in A, 1 in MC; rep from * three more times, p1 in MC, 4 in A, SM, p1 in MC, 4 in A, 1 in MC, SM, p4 in A, 1 in MC, *1 in MC, 4 in A, 1 in MC; rep from * two more times, k1 in MC.

MITTEN (MAKE 2)

Using 2.75mm (US 2) needles and MC, CO 57 sts.

Work in k1, p1 rib for 6cm (2½in) dec one st at end of last row (56 sts).

Change to 3.25mm (US 3) needles and St st.

THUMB GUSSET

Starting at Row 1, work from chart as follows:

Row 1 (RS): Patt 24, PM, m1, k2, m1, PM, patt to end.

Row 2: Patt 30, SM, patt 4, SM, patt to end.

Row 3: Patt 24, SM, m1, patt 4, m1, SM, patt to end.

Row 4: Patt 30, SM, patt 6, SM, patt to end.

Row 5: Patt 24, SM, m1, patt 6, m1, SM, patt to end.

Row 6: Patt 30, SM, patt 8, SM, patt to end.

Row 7: Patt 24, SM, m1, patt to next marker, m1, SM, patt to end.

Row 8: Patt 30, SM, patt to next marker, SM, patt to end.

Rep last two rows a further six times until Row 20 of chart has

been worked and there are 22 sts between the two markers.

THUMB

Row 1: In MC, k46, turn, CO 2 sts. Starting at Row 2 (WS), work from chart as follows:

Row 2: Patt 24 (including two newly CO sts), turn, CO 2 sts (in D).

Rows 3 to 19: Starting with a knit row, work 17 rows on these 26 sts until Row 19 has been completed.

SHAPE TOP

Row 20 (WS): *P2tog in MC, p1 in MC, p2tog in D, p1 in MC; rep from * three more times, p2tog in MC (17 sts). Break off all contrast colours and cont in MC only.

Row 21: K1, *k2tog; rep from * to end of row (9 sts).

Break off yarn, thread through rem sts, draw up and fasten off.

Sew seam.

MAIN SECTION (BOTH MITTENS)

Row 1: With RS facing, rejoin yarn (MC), pick up and knit 2 sts at base of thumb and knit to end of row (56 sts).

Rows 2 to 20: Starting with Row 2 (WS row), work 19 rows of chart until Row 20 has been completed.

SHAPE TOP

Rows 21 to 34: Follow chart from Row 21 to Row 34.

Row 35: K1 in MC, k2tog tbl in MC, patt 23, k2tog in C, K2tog tbl in C, patt 23, k2tog in MC, k1 in MC.

Row 36: Work Row 16 of chart (all in MC).

Row 37: K1in MC, k2tog tbl in MC, patt 21, k2tog in D, k2tog tbl in D, patt 21, k2tog in MC, k1.

Row 38: Work Row 18 of chart.

Row 39: K1 in MC, k2tog tbl in MC, patt 19, k2tog in D, k2tog tbl in D, patt 19, k2tog in MC, k1 in MC.

Row 40: Work Row 20 of chart.

Row 41 (all in MC): K1, k2tog tbl, k17, k2tog, k2tog tbl, k17, k2tog, k1.

Row 42: Work Row 2 of chart.

Row 43: K1 in MC, k2tog tbl, patt 15, k2tog in A, k2tog tbl in A, patt 15, k2tog in MC, k1 in MC.

Row 44: Patt 16, p2tog tbl in A, p2tog in A, slip this st back to LH needle. Graft two sets of sts together, changing colour according to sts being grafted. Alternatively, turn mitten inside out and double cast off.

FINISHING

Darn in loose ends.

Pin out according to measurement diagram. Steam or press very lightly using a pressing cloth, avoiding the ribbing.

Sew side seam.

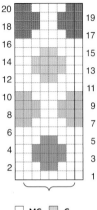

☐ MC ☐ C
▨ A   ▨ D
▨ B

ON THE SPOT

Why not use a darker colour for the main colour (MC) of the mitten and add white or cream spots to complement it?

Slip Stitch Wrist-Warmers

Break out of the box with these desirable wrist-warmers made using a luxurious alpaca silk mix. Try knitting these on needles the next size up to make them larger. Designed by Jennifer L. Appleby.

YARN

Debbie Bliss *Alpaca Silk Aran* (80% alpaca, 20% silk), approx. 50g/105m per ball
- 1 ball of Berry 12 **(MC)**
- 1 ball of Pink 20 **(A)**

NEEDLES

Set of 5.00mm (US 8) double-pointed knitting needles (dpns)

TENSION

18 sts and 23 rows = 10cm (4in) square measured over St st using 5.00mm (US 8) needles.

TO FIT

One size

SKILL LEVEL

Intermediate

DOTTED BOX SLIP STITCH PATTERN

Worked over 10 rounds.

NOTE: Work all slip stitches with yarn in back of work.

Round 1: With A, *sl1, k5, sl1, k1; rep from * to end of round.

Round 2: With A, *sl1, p5, sl1, p1; rep from * to end of round.

Round 3: With MC, k1, *sl1, k3; rep from * to last 3 sts; sl1, k2.

Round 4: Rep Round 3.

Round 5: With A, k2, *sl1, k1, sl1, k5; rep from * to last 6 sts; sl1, k1, sl1, k3.

Round 6: With A, p2, *sl1, p1, sl1, p5; rep from * to last 6 sts; sl1, p1, sl1, p3.

Rounds 7–8: Rep Rounds 3–4.

Rounds 9–10: Rep Rounds 1–2.

HAMMERHEAD STRIPE SLIP STITCH PATTERN

Worked over 10 rounds.

NOTE: Work all slip stitches with yarn in back of work.

Round 1: With A, k1, *sl1, k3; rep from * to last 3 sts; sl1, k2.

Round 2: With A, p1, *sl1, p3; rep from * to last 3 sts; sl1, p2.

Round 3: With MC, *k3, sl1; rep from * to end of round.

Round 4: Rep Round 3.

Round 5: With A, knit.

Round 6: With A, purl.

Rounds 7–8: Rep Rounds 3–4.

Rounds 9–10: Rep Rounds 1–2.

RIGHT MITT

Using A, CO 32 sts. Divide on to three dpns: 12, 8, 12 sts.

Rounds 1–5: Work in k2, p2 rib.

Rounds 6–8: With MC, knit.

Rounds 9–18: Work Dotted Box Slip Stitch Pattern.

Rounds 19–21: Rep Rounds 6–8.

Rounds 22–31: Work Hammerhead Stripe Slip Stitch Pattern.

Rounds 32–34: Rep Rounds 6–8.

Rounds 35–44: Work Dotted Box Slip Stitch Pattern.

Round 45: With MC, knit.

MAKE THUMB OPENING

Round 46: With MC, k15. With a 30cm (12in) length of contrasting waste yarn, knit the next 5 sts; replace these 5 sts on LH needle; with MC, knit across these same 5 sts, knit to end of round.

Round 47: With MC, knit.

Rounds 48–57: Work Hammerhead Stripe Slip Stitch Pattern.

Rounds 58–60: Rep Rounds 6–8.

Round 61: With A, knit.

Rounds 62–65: With A, work in k2, p2 rib.

Round 66: Cast off LOOSELY in pattern.

THUMB

Carefully remove waste yarn at thumb opening, and place the 5 sts at the top of the opening on one dpn, and the 5 sts at the bottom of the opening on another dpn. Pick up an extra st on each side of thumb opening to make a total of 12 sts. Divide sts on to three dpns: 4, 4, 4 sts.

With MC, knit 2 rounds. Break MC.

With A, knit 1 round, then work 4 rounds in k2, p2 rib.

Cast off LOOSELY in pattern.

LEFT MITT

Work as for Right Mitt to Round 45.

MAKE THUMB OPENING

Round 46: With MC, k10. With a 30cm (12in) length of contrasting waste yarn, knit the next 5 sts; replace these 5 sts on LH needle; with MC, knit across these same 5 sts, knit to end of round. Work remainder of Left Mitt as for Right Mitt.

FINISHING

Darn in all ends, making sure that you close up any holes around the base of the thumbs.

Textured Gloves

These easy-going gloves take you from day to night
without missing a beat. Designed by Gosia Dzik-Holden.

YARN

Debbie Bliss *Alpaca Silk DK* (80% alpaca, 20% silk), approx. 50g/105m per ball
4 balls of Yellow 15

NEEDLES

Set of 2.00mm (US 0) double-pointed needles (dpns)
Cable needle

TENSION

14 sts and 16 rows = 5cm (2in) square measured over St st using
2.00mm (US 0) needles.

TO FIT

One size

SKILL LEVEL

Advanced

SPECIAL ABBREVIATIONS

See page 95 for information on MB (make bobble).

SCHIAPARELLI STITCH

Worked in rounds over an even number of sts.

Crossed st (Cr st): Insert RH needle through the front loop of the first st from right to left and then knit the second st through front loop in one motion from this position, taking the second stitch off the needle, then knit the first st still on the needle tbl.

Round 1: *Work Cr st over next 2 sts; rep from * to end.

Rounds 2 and 4: Knit.

Round 3: K1, *work Cr st over next 2 sts; rep from *, end k1.

Rep Rounds 1–4.

GLOVES
ARM (MAKE 2)

Using 2.00mm (US 0) dpns and long-tail/Continental method, CO 64 sts on one needle. Divide sts evenly on to four needles (16 sts per needle). Join for working in the round, being careful not to twist sts, and PM after first st to denote beg of round. Knit one round.

Round 1: *P1, k1, p1, MB; rep from * to end.

Rounds 2 and 3: *P1, k1; rep from * to end.

Rounds 4 and 5: Knit.

Cable round: Place 2 sts on cn and hold at back of work, k2, k2 sts from

cn, *work Cr st over next 2 sts; rep from * to end.

Round 7: Knit.

Round 8: K5, *work Cr st over next 2 sts; rep from * to last st, k1.

Round 9: Knit.

Cable round: As Round 6.

Round 11: As Round 7.

Round 12: As Round 8.

Round 13: Knit to last st, slip last st to RH needle.

Cable and dec round: Place 2 sts on cn and hold at back of work, transfer slipped st from RH needle to LH needle; k2tog, k1, k1 st from cn, transfer second st knitwise from cn to RH needle, k1, psso, k1, *work Cr st over next 2 sts; rep from * to last st; k1.

Round 15: Knit.

Round 16: K4, *work Cr st over next 2 sts; rep from * to end.

Round 17: Knit.

Cable round: Place 2 sts on cn and hold at back of work, k2, k2 sts from cn, k1, *work Cr st over next 2 sts; rep from * to last st, k1.

Round 19: Knit.

Round 20: K4, *work Cr st over next 2 sts; rep from * to end.

Round 21: Knit to last st, slip to RH needle.

Cable and dec round: Place 2 sts on cn and hold at back of work, transfer

slipped st from RH needle to LH needle; k2tog, k1, k1 st from cn, slip second st from cn to RH needle, k1, psso, *work Cr st over next 2 sts; rep from * to end of round.

Rep Rounds 7–22 four more times (44 sts).

Work 11 rounds even.

Rounds 1–6: As Rounds 7–12.

Round 7: Knit.

Cable round: Place 2 sts on cn and hold at back of work, k2, k2 sts from cn, *work Cr st over next 2 sts; rep from * to end.

Round 9: Knit.

Round 10: K5, *work Cr st over next 2 sts; rep from * to last st, k1.

Round 11: Knit.

Cable round: Place 2 sts on cn and hold at back of work, k2, k2 sts from cn, *work Cr st over next 2 sts; rep from * to end. Work should measure about 25.5cm (10in).

Inc round: K4, [m1, k1], k to last st, [k1, m1].

RIGHT HAND
SHAPE THUMB

Next round: K4, *work Cr st over next 2 sts; rep from * nine more times.

THUMB SECTION (TS)

Place next 6 sts on sep needle, knit these 6 sts, knit to end of round.

Next round: Knit.

Cable round: Place 2 sts on cn and hold at back of work, k2, k2 sts from cn, k1, *work Cr st over next 2 sts; rep from * eight more times, k1; **TS:** k6; knit to end.

Inc round: K4, [m1, k1], knit to last st, [k1, m1].

Thumb inc round: K5, *work Cr st over next 2 sts; rep from * nine more times; **TS:** [k1, m1], k4, [m1, k1]; knit to end of round.

Next round: Knit.

Cable round: Place 2 sts on cn and hold at back of work, k2, k2 sts from cn, *work Cr st over next 2 sts; rep from * nine more times, k1; **TS:** k8; knit to end.

Inc round: K4, [m1, k1], knit to last st, [k1, m1].

Next round: K4, *work Cr st over next 2 sts; rep from * ten more times, knit to end.

Thumb inc round: K26; **TS:** [k1, m1], k6, [m1, k1]; knit to end.

Cable round: Place 2 sts on cn and hold at back of work, k2, k2 sts from cn, k1, *work Cr st over next 2 sts; rep from * nine more times, k1; **TS:** k10; knit to end.

Inc round: K4, [m1, k1], knit to last st, [k1, m1].

Next round: K5, *work Cr st over next 2 sts; rep from * ten more times, knit to end.

Next round: Knit.

Thumb inc and cable round: Place 2 sts on cn and hold at back of work, k2, k2 sts from cn; *work Cr st over next 2 sts; rep from * ten more times, k1. **TS:** [k1, m1], k8, [m1, k1]; knit to end.

Inc round: K4, [m1, k1], knit to last st, [k1, m1] (60 sts).

Next round: K4, *work Cr st over next 2 sts; rep from * eleven more times; knit to end.

Next round: Knit.

Cable round: Place 2 sts on cn and hold at back of work, k2, k2 sts from cn; k1, *work Cr st over next 2 sts; rep from * ten more times, k1; knit to end.

Next round: K28.

TS: K6, take new needle and knit rem 6 sts of TS, take another new needle and CO 6 sts using loop method; close work and cont in St st until approx. 0.75cm (⅜in) less than desired length is reached.

Next round: [K2tog, k1] six times (12 sts).

Next round: Knit.

Next round: K2tog to end (6 sts).

PALM OF HAND

Pick up 9 sts along the line of thumb, CO for the thumb and knit to end of round (57 sts).

Next round: K4, *work Cr st over next 2 sts; rep from * eleven more times; knit to end.

Next round: Knit to last st, slip last st to RH needle.

Cable and dec round: Place 2 sts on cn and hold at back of work, transfer slipped st from RH needle to LH needle, k2tog, k1, k1 st from cn, slip second st knitwise from cn to RH needle, k1, psso, *work Cr st over next 2 sts; rep from * ten more times; knit to end of round.

Next round: Knit.

Next round: K5, *work Cr st over next 2 sts; rep from * ten more times; knit to end.

Next round: Knit to last st, slip last st to RH needle.

Cable and dec round: Place 2 sts on cn and hold at back of work, transfer slipped st from RH needle to LH needle; k2tog, k1, k1 st from cn, slip second st knitwise from cn to RH needle, k1, psso; k1, *work Cr st over next 2 sts; rep from * nine more times; knit to end of round (47 sts).

Next round: Knit.

Next round: K4, *work Cr st over next 2 sts; rep from * ten more times; knit to end.

Next round: Knit to last st, slip last st to RH needle.

Rep last 8 rounds once more.

NOTE: Number of reps of Cr sts diminishes as sts on needle are dec (i.e. in third dec round work Cr st nine times in total, in fourth dec round work it eight times in total). Make sure you have a neat line between pattern and St st on inside of hand.

Cable and dec round: Place 2 sts on cn and hold at back of work, transfer slipped st from RH needle to LH needle; k2tog, k1, k1 st from cn, slip second st knitwise from cn to RH needle, k1, psso, *work Cr st over next 2 sts; rep from * ten more times; knit to end of round (47 sts).

Next round: Knit.

FINGERS

On finishing last round, k first 2 sts of cable and then split 47 sts in two and place them on two needles (2 sts of cable on each needle).

LITTLE FINGER

Knit first 6 sts of round; using loop method, CO 3 sts on new needle; transfer 6 sts of the last round to spare needle. Slip one st from each needle to one with newly CO sts [5 sts on each needle] (15 sts).

Work these 15 sts in round until you reach 3 rounds fewer than desired length.

Next round: [K2tog, k1] to end.

Next round: Knit.

Next round: K2tog to end.

Cast off.

THIRD FINGER

Pick up 3 sts CO for little finger, k5 along upper side of hand, CO 4 sts, k5 along inner side of hand (17 sts).

Work as for little finger.

SECOND FINGER

Pick up 4 sts CO for third finger, k5 along upper side of hand, CO 4 sts, k5 along inner side of hand (18 sts).

Work as for little finger.

FIRST FINGER

Pick up 4 sts CO for second finger, k15 along upper and inner side of hand (19 sts).

Work as for little finger.

LEFT HAND

SHAPE THUMB

Next round: K20.

THUMB SECTION (TS)

Place next 6 sts on sep needle, knit these 6 sts and then *work Cr st over next 2 sts; rep from * nine more times.

Next round: Knit.

Cable round: Place 2 sts on cn and hold at back of work, k2, k2 sts from cn, k23, *work Cr st over next 2 sts; rep from * eight more times, k1.

Inc round: K4, [m1, k1], knit to last st, [k1, m1].

Thumb inc round: K21; **TS:** [k1, m1], k4, [m1, k1], *work Cr st over next 2 sts; rep from * nine more times, k1.

Next round: Knit.

Cable round: Place 2 sts on cn and hold at back of work, k2, k2 sts from cn, k26, *work Cr st over next 2 sts; rep from * nine more times.

Inc round: K4, [m1, k1], knit to last st, [k1, m1].

Next round: K30, *work Cr st over next 2 sts; rep from * ten more times.

Thumb inc round: K22; **TS:** [k1, m1], k6, [m1, k1]; knit to end.

Cable round: Place 2 sts on cn and hold at back of work, k2, k2 sts from cn, k29, *work Cr st over next 2 sts; rep from * nine more times, k1.

Inc round: K4, [m1, k1], knit to last st, [k1, m1].

Next round: K33, *work Cr st over next 2 sts; rep from * ten more times, k1.

Next round: Knit.

Thumb inc and cable round: Place 2 sts on cn and hold at back of work, k2, k2 sts from cn; k19; **TS:** [k1, m1], k8, [m1, k1]; k1, *work Cr st over next 2 sts; rep from * ten more times (2 sts inc).

Inc round: K4, [m1, k1], knit to last st, [k1, m1] (60 sts).

Next round: K36, *work Cr st over next 2 sts; rep from * eleven more times.

Next round: Knit.

Cable round: Place 2 sts on cn and hold at back of work, k2, k2 sts from cn; k33, *work Cr st over next 2 sts; rep from * ten more times, k1.

Next round: K24.

TS: K6, take new needle and knit rem 6 sts of TS, then take yet another needle and CO 6 sts using loop method; close

work and cont in St st until approx. 0.75cm (⅜in) less than desired length.

Next round: [K2tog, k1] six times (12 sts).

Next round: Knit.

Next round: K2tog to end (6 sts).

PALM OF HAND

Pick up 9 sts along the line of thumb CO and then knit to end of round (57 sts).

Next round: K33, *work Cr st over next 2 sts; rep from * eleven more times.

Next round: Knit to last st, slip last st to RH needle.

Cable and dec round: Place 2 sts on cn and hold at back of work, transfer slipped st from RH needle to LH needle; k2tog, k1, k1 from cn, slip second st knitwise from cn to RH needle, k1, psso; k29, *work Cr st over next 2 sts; rep from * ten more times.

Next round: Knit.

Next round: K32, *work Cr st over next 2 sts; rep from * ten more times; k1.

Next round: Knit to last st, slip last st to RH needle.

Cable and dec round: Place 2 sts on cn and hold at back of work, transfer slipped st from RH needle to LH needle; k2tog, k1, k1 st from cn, slip second st knitwise from cn to RH needle, k1, psso; k28, *work Cr st over next 2 sts; rep from * nine more times; k1.

Next round: Knit.

Next round: K31, *work Cr st over next 2 sts; rep from * ten more times.

Next round: Knit to last st, slip last st to RH needle.

Cable and dec round: Place 2 sts on cn and hold at back of work, transfer slipped st from RH needle to LH needle; k2tog, k1, k1 st from cn, slip second st knitwise from cn to RH needle, k1, psso; k27, *work Cr st over next 2 sts; rep from * nine more times.

Next round: Knit.

Next round: K30, *work Cr st over next 2 sts; rep from * nine more times; k1.

Next round: Knit to last st, slip last st to RH needle.

Cable and dec round: Place 2 sts on cn and hold at back of work, transfer slipped st from RH needle to LH needle; k2tog, k1, k1 st from cn, slip second st knitwise from cn to RH needle, k1, psso; k26, *work Cr st over next 2 sts; rep from * eight more times; k1.

Next round: Knit.

Next round: K29, *work Cr st over next 2 sts; rep from * nine more times.

Next round: Knit to last st, slip last st to RH needle.

Cable and dec round: Place 2 sts on cn and hold at back of work, transfer sl st from RH needle to LH needle; k2tog, k1, k1 st from cn, slip second st knitwise from cn to RH needle, k1, psso, k25, *work Cr st over next 2 sts; rep from * eight more times (47 sts).

Next round: Knit.

FINGERS

On finishing last round, k2 first sts off cable and then split 47 sts and place on two needles (2 sts of cable on each needle).

LITTLE FINGER

Knit first 7 sts of round; using loop method, CO 3 sts to new needle; transfer last 7 sts of the last round to spare needle. Slip one st from each needle to one with newly CO sts [5 sts on each needle] (15 sts).

Work these 17 sts in round until you reach 3 rounds fewer than desired length.

Next round: [K2tog, k1] to end.

Next round: Knit.

Next round: K2tog to end. Cast off.

THIRD FINGER

Pick up 3 sts CO for little finger, k5 along upper side of hand, CO 4 sts, k5 along inner side of hand (17 sts).

Work as for little finger.

SECOND FINGER

Pick up 4 sts CO for little finger, k5 along upper side of hand, CO 4 sts, k5 along inner side of hand (18 sts).

Work as for little finger.

FIRST FINGER

Pick up 4 sts CO for middle finger, k15 along upper and inner side of hand (19 sts).

Work as for little finger.

FINISHING

When you finish, turn the gloves inside out and weave in all the ends. Turn the gloves right side out again. Soak overnight in soapy water, then rinse thoroughly in tepid water to which a few drops of lavender oil have been added (optional).

ROUND UP

- After working first round, transfer one st to each side of new CO ones from neighbouring needles – to avoid irregular sts in these areas.
- Make sure that the thread goes through small thumb opening. Once the thumb is finished, you can then run the thread inside it to pick up work on the palm of hand directly and without having to weave in loose ends.

Rose-Button Gauntlets

These charming hand-warmers are simple to make in double crochet. The pretty lace panel at the wrist is decorated with a row of small crocheted rose buttons. Designed by Claire Garland.

YARN

Lana Grossa *Royal Tweed* (100% wool), approx. 50g/100m per ball

   1 ball of Pink 26 **(MC)**

   1 ball of Tangerine 21 **(A)**

RYC *Cashcotton 4-ply* (35% cotton, 25% polyamide, 18% angora, 13% viscose, 9% cashmere), approx. 50g/180m per ball

   1 ball of Pretty 902 **(B)**

HOOK	**NEEDLE**
One 5.50mm (I/9) crochet hook	Large-eyed yarn needle

TENSION

11 sts and 13 rows = 10cm (4in) square measured over double crochet using 5.50mm (I/9) hook.

TO FIT	**SKILL LEVEL**
One size	Beginner/ intermediate

GAUNTLET

RIGHT GAUNTLET

Foundation chain (RS): Using A and 5.50mm (I/9) hook, beg at the cuff end and make 24ch plus 1ch as tch, turn.

Row 1 (WS): 1dc in each 24ch across, 1ch, turn.

Row 2 (RS): 1dc in each 24dc across, 1ch, turn.

Rep last row three times more, ending with ss in last dc to fasten off A, turn.

Row 6 (RS): Join on MC to ss (counts as first st), 1ch, 1dc in each 23dc across, 1ch, turn.

Row 7 (WS): 1dc in each 23dc across, ending 1dc in ss, 1ch, turn.

Row 8 (RS): 1dc in each 24dc across, 1ch, turn.

Rep last row five times more, join with ss in first dc (does not count as st) to form ring and cont to work in rounds (24 dc).

Round 1 (RS): Miss ss, 1dc in each 24dc around, ss in first sc.

Rep last round twice more.

ADD THUMB

Round 4: 2dc in next dc, 1dc in each next 23dc (25 dc).

Rep last round, inc 1dc into first dc of each of next three rounds (28 dc).

SHAPE THUMB

Round 8: 2dc in next dc, 1dc in each next 3dc, miss next 20dc, 1dc in each next 4dc [this shapes the thumb] (9 dc).

Cont to work on the thumb only.

Round 9: 1dc in each next 9dc.

Rep last round once more.

Fasten off.

HAND

Join on A to rem 20dc to st at inside edge of thumb, cont to work in rounds to complete the hand.

Round 1: 2dc in next dc, 1dc in each next 20dc (21 dc).

Round 2: 1dc in each next 21dc. Rep last round four times more. Fasten off.

Make Left Gauntlet in same way.

LACY EDGING

RIGHT GAUNTLET

With front of glove uppermost (thumb facing out towards right), using 5.50mm (I/9) hook join on yarn B with ss to dc beneath thumb at opening on right front edge.

Row 1: 1ch, 1dc in each next 13dc down to cuff on right edge opening, 1ch, turn (13 dc).

Row 2 (WS): Miss first dc, 1dc in each next dc, ending 1dc in 1ch, 1ch, turn.

Row 3: Miss first dc, *miss 1dc, 5tr in next dc, skip 1dc, 1dc in next dc; rep from *, ending 1dc last dc.

Fasten off.

LEFT GAUNTLET

With front of glove uppermost (thumb facing out towards left), using 5.50mm (I/9) hook join on yarn B with ss to dc beneath thumb at opening on left front edge. Work as for Right Gauntlet, but on left edge opening.

ROSE BUTTON

Foundation row: Using yarn MC and 5.50mm (I/9) hook, make 4ch.

Round 1: 10dc in fourth ch from hook, working over loose end.

Fasten off, leave a tail of yarn for sewing it to the gauntlet.

Make three more alike in yarn C, and two in yarn MC.

FINISHING

Use the buttons to join the opening in the gauntlet. Sew three buttons in order: one pink at cuff, then two tangerine, evenly spaced, to front of lacy edging. When buttons are in position, turn glove inside out and secure yarn at back. Weave in all ends.

Driving Gloves

These flirty, openwork gloves are knitted with an incredibly soft blend of lambswool and mohair, and will add a touch of luxury to even the shortest trip. Designed by Carol Meldrum.

YARN

Rowan *Kid Classic* (70% lambswool, 26% kid mohair, 4% nylon), approx. 50g/140m per ball
   3 balls of Victoria 852

NEEDLES	**BUTTONS**

Pair of 6.50mm (US 8) knitting needles	Two buttons of prefered colour and size

---

TENSION

---

20 sts and 20 rows = 10cm (4in) square measured over patt on 6.50mm (US 8) needles.

TO FIT	**SKILL LEVEL**

One size	Intermediate

LEFT GLOVE

With 6.50mm (US 8) needles, CO 20 sts.

Row 1: Knit.

Row 2: Purl.

Row 3: K2tog, [yo] twice, k2tog, yo, k12, yo, sl1, k1, psso, [yo] twice, sl1, k1, psso (22 sts).

Row 4: P1, purl into first yo and knit into second yo of prev row, p16, purl into first yo and knit into second yo of prev row, p1.

Row 5: K2tog, [yo] twice, k2tog, yo, k14, yo, sl1, k1, psso, [yo] twice, sl1, k1, psso (24 sts).

Row 6: P1, purl into first yo and knit into second yo of prev row, p18, purl into first of yo and knit into second yo of prev row, p1.

Row 7: K2tog, [yo] twice, k2tog, yo, k16, yo, sl1, k1, psso, [yo] twice, sl1, k1, psso (26 sts).

Row 8: P1, purl into first yo and knit into second yo of prev row, p20, purl into first yo and knit into second yo of prev row, p1.

Row 9: Cast off 3 sts, knit to end (23 sts).

Row 10: Cast off 3sts, purl to end (20 sts).

Rows 3–10 form lace edge pattern. Keep lace pattern correct throughout.

PLACE THUMB

Row 11: K2tog, [yo] twice, k2tog, yo, k9, turn (14 sts).

Work on these 14 sts only, slip rem sts on to stitch holder.

Row 12: K1, p11, k1, p1.

Row 13: K2tog, [yo] twice, k2tog, yo, knit to end, turn (16 sts).

Row 14: K1, p12, k1, p1.

Row 15: K2tog, [yo] twice, k2tog, yo, knit to end, turn (16 sts).

Row 16: K1, p13, k1, p1.

Row 17: Cast off 3 sts at beg of row, knit to end (13 sts).

Break off yarn and rejoin to rest of sts.

Next row: K3, yo, sl1, k1, psso, [yo] twice, sl1, k1, psso (8 sts).

Next row: P2, k1, p4, k1.

Next row: K4, yo, sl1, k1, psso, [yo] twice, sl1, k1, psso (9 sts).

Next row: P2, k1, p5, k1.

Next row: K5, yo, sl1, k1, psso, [yo] twice, sl1, k1, psso (10 sts).

Next row: P2, k1, p6, k1.

Break off yarn.

Rejoin two sides tog to close thumb hole, work foll row with yarn from RH needle.

Next row: Cast off 3 sts at beg of row, purl to end.

Rep Rows 3–9 once more.

Next row: Knit.

Cast off purlwise.

RIGHT GLOVE

Work as for Left Glove until thumb.

PLACE THUMB

Row 11: K2tog, [yo] twice, k2tog, yo, k3, turn (8 sts).

Work on these 8 sts only, slip rem sts on to stitch holder.

Row 12: K1, p5, k1, p1.

Row 13: K2tog, [yo] twice, k2tog, yo, knit to end, turn (9 sts).

Row 14: K1, p6, k1, p1.

Row 15: K2tog, [yo] twice, k2tog, yo, knit to end, turn (10 sts).

Row 16: K1, p7, k1, p1.

Row 17: Cast off 3 sts at beg of row, knit to end (7 sts).

Break off yarn and rejoin to rest of sts.

Next row: Knit to last 4 sts, yo, sl1, k1, psso, [yo] twice, sl1, k1, psso (14 sts).

Next row: P2, k1, purl to last st, k1.

Next row: Knit to last 4 sts, yo, sl1, k1, psso, [yo] twice, sl1, k1, psso (15 sts).

Next row: P2, k1, purl to last st, k1.

Next row: Knit to last 4 sts, yo, sl1, k1, psso, [yo] twice, sl1, k1, psso (16 sts).

Next row: P2, k1, purl to last st, k1.

Break off yarn.

Rejoin two sides tog to close thumb hole, work foll row with yarn from RH needle.

Next row: Cast off 3 sts at beg of row, purl to end.

Rep Rows 3–9 once more.

Next row: Knit.

Cast off purlwise.

FINISHING

Catch widest part of gloves together at back of hand. Make a buttonhole at cast-on edge and sew button to correspond.

ON THE BALL

Use two ends of yarn together throughout – take one end from centre of ball and the other from the outside and knit together.

Sequined Mittens

Sparkly sequins lend a fun and playful touch to these sumptuous mohair mittens designed by Melissa Halvorson. Alternatively, an array of beads in technicolours are just as pretty.

YARN

Rowan *Kidsilk Haze* (70% kid mohair, 30% silk), approx. 25g/210m per ball
  1 ball of Splendour 579 **(A)**
Rowan *Kid Classic* (70% lambswool, 26% kid mohair, 4% nylon) approx. 50g/140m per ball
  1 ball of Frilly 844 **(B)**

NEEDLES

One 5.00mm (US 8) 30cm (12in) circular knitting needle
Set 5.00mm (US 8) double-pointed needles (dpns)

SEQUINS

Approx. 500 x 6mm (¼in) sequins

TENSION

16 sts and 22 rows = 10cm (4in) square measured over St st using 5.00mm (US 8) needles.

TO FIT	SKILL LEVEL
One size	Beginner

DUPLICATE STITCH

Bring the threaded yarn needle through the back just below the stitch you would like to cover. In one motion, pick up a sequin and insert the needle under both loops one row above and pull it through, anchoring the sequin to one side of the stitch. Pick up a second sequin and insert the needle back into the stitch below.

MITTEN (MAKE 2)

Using one strand of each yarn, CO 30 sts.
PM at join.
Work in K2, p1 rib for 10cm (4in) or desired length of gauntlet.
Next round: Knit to marker, SM, k2, PM.
Next round: Knit to marker (2 sts between markers).

THUMB GUSSET

Next round: SM, m1, k2, m1, SM, complete round (4 sts between markers).
Knit 2 rounds.
Next round: SM, m1, k4, m1, SM, complete round.
Knit 2 rounds.
Cont in this manner until there are 12 sts between the markers.
Next round (to make up for the 2 sts used for the gusset): Knit to marker, m1, SM, knit across 12 sts, place these 12 sts on stitch holder, remove marker, m1.

PALM

Knit 10 rows.
Row 11: SM, k15, PM, k15.
If using cuff-size circular needles, switch to dpns at this point.
Rows 12, 14, 16, 18, 20, 22: *Knit to 2 sts before marker, k2tog tbl, SM, k2tog; rep from * once more.
Rows 13, 15, 17, 19, 21: Knit.
When only 6 sts are left, thread yarn through twice in a clockwise motion and grip. Thread yarn through centre of the gripped stitches and pull inside.

THUMB

Pick up the 12 thumb sts with dpns, twisting the 2 sts closest to the join with the palm to prevent a gap.
Work in St st for 10 rows or desired length of thumb.
Row 11: K2tog so that 6 sts rem.
Finish as for the top of the mitten.

FINISHING

With remaining 6 sts, thread yarn through twice in a clockwise motion and grip. Thread yarn through centre of gripped stitches and pull inside.

Eyelet Arm-Warmers

Long and elegant, a simple eyelet detail adorns the length of the arm-warmer for a spectacular look. They can also be knitted as mittens with just a few extra steps. Designed by Lynn Serpe.

YARN

Rowan *4-ply Soft* (100% merino wool), approx. 50g/175m per ball
  1 ball of Sooty 372

NEEDLES

Four 2.75mm (US 2) double-pointed needles (dpns)
Four 2.25mm (US 1) double-pointed needles (dpns)

TENSION

28 sts and 36 rows = 10cm (4in) square measured over St st using 2.75mm (US 2) needles

TO FIT	SKILL LEVEL
One size	Intermediate

RIGHT ARM-WARMER

Using 2.75mm (US 2) dpns, CO 60 sts.

Round 1: Knit, dividing sts evenly on three dpns.

Round 2: Join for working in the round (being careful not to twist), knit.

Rounds 3–4: Knit.

Round 5: Purl.

Round 6: [Yo, k2tog] to end of round.

Round 7: Purl.

Rounds 8–11: Knit.

Round 12: Fold CO edge under and make hem by knitting tog the CO round and the active round as follows: using 2.25mm (US 1) needles, pick up first CO st with right needle and place it on left needle, k2tog, cont for entire round picking up the next CO st and knitting it tog with next active st.

Rounds 13–15: Using 2.75mm (US 2) needles, knit.

Round 16: K2tog, knit to end of round.

Rounds 17–19: Knit.

Round 20: Knit to last 2 sts, ssk (58 sts).

Round 21: Purl.

Round 22: [Yo, k2tog] to end of rnd.

Round 23: Purl.

Round 24: K2tog, knit to end of rnd.

Rounds 25–27: Knit.

Round 28: Knit to last 2 sts, ssk (56 sts).

BEGIN PATTERNING

Round 29: K13, [k2tog, yo, k12] twice, k2tog, yo, k13.

Round 30: K12, [k2tog, yo, k1, yo, ssk, k9] twice, k2tog, yo, k1, yo, ssk, k11.

Round 31: Knit.

Round 32: K2tog, knit to end of rnd.

Rounds 33–35: Knit.

Round 36: Knit to last 2 sts, ssk (54 sts).

Round 37: K5, [k2tog, yo, k12] three times, k2tog, yo, k5.

Round 38: K4, [k2tog, yo, k1, yo, ssk, k9] three times, k2tog, yo, k1, yo, ssk, k3.

Rounds 39–44: Rep Rounds 31-36 (52 sts).

Round 45: K11, [k2tog, yo, k12] twice, k2tog, yo, k11.

Round 46: K10, [k2tog, yo, k1, yo, ssk, k9] three times.

Rounds 47-52: Rep Rounds 31-36 (50 sts).

Round 53: K3, [k2tog, yo, k12] three times, k2tog, yo, k3.

Round 54: K2, [k2tog, yo, k1, yo, ssk, k9] three times, k2tog, yo, k1, yo, ssk, k1.

Rounds 55–60: Rep Rounds 31-36 (48 sts).

Round 61: K9, [k2tog, yo, k12] twice, k2tog, yo, k9.

Round 62: K8, [k2tog, yo, k1, yo, ssk, k9] twice, k2tog, yo, k1, yo, ssk, k7.

Rounds 63-68: Rep Rounds 31-36 (46 sts).

Round 69: Yo, k14 [k2tog, yo, k12] twice, k2, k2tog.

Round 70: K1, yo, ssk, k11 [k2tog, yo, k1, yo, ssk, k9] twice, k2, k2tog, yo.

Rounds 71-76: Rep Rounds 31-36 (44 sts).

Round 77: K7, [k2tog, yo, k12] twice, k2tog, yo, k7.

Round 78: K6, [k2tog, yo, k1, yo, ssk, k9] twice, k2tog, yo, k1, yo, ssk, k5.

Rounds 79-84: Rep Rounds 31-36 (42 sts).

FOR SHORTER LENGTH

Skip the next 16 rounds and go to the Hand section.

FOR LONGER LENGTH

Round 85: Yo, k12 [k2tog, yo, k12] twice, k2tog.

Round 86: K1, yo, ssk, k9 [k2tog, yo, k1, yo, ssk, k9] twice, k2tog, yo.

Rounds 87–92: Knit.

Round 93: K6, [k2tog, yo, k12] twice, k2tog, yo, k6.

Round 94: K5, [k2tog, yo, k1, yo, ssk, k9] twice, k2tog, yo, k1, yo, ssk, k4.

Rounds 95-100: Knit.

UPPER HAND

Round 1: [K13, yo, k1, yo] three times (48 sts).

Rounds 2–8: Knit.

Round 9: K6, [yo, k1, yo, k15] twice, yo, k1, yo, k9 (54 sts).

Rounds 10–16: Knit.

Round 17: [K17, yo, k1, yo] three times (60 sts).

Rounds 18–19: Knit.

UPPER HAND HEM

Rounds 20–22: Knit.

Round 23: Purl.

Round 24: [Yo, k2tog] to end of rnd.

Round 25: Purl.

Rounds 26–28: Knit.

Round 29: Make hem by knitting together the back of Round 20 (three rounds before the first purl round) and the active round as follows: using 2.25mm (US 1) needles to pick up the back of the first st of Round 20 with right needle and place it on left needle, K2tog, cont for entire round picking up the back of the next st of Round 20 and knitting it tog with next active st.

FOR FULL MITTENS
RIGHT HAND

Round 1: Using 2.75mm (US 2) needles, k40, PM, k10, PM, k10.

Round 2 (inc): Knit to first marker, SM, m1r, knit to next marker, m1l, SM, knit to end of rnd (12 sts bet markers for thumb).

Round 3: Knit.

Round 4: Rep Round 2 (14 sts bet markers).

Round 5: Knit.

Round 6: Rep Round 2 (16 sts between markers).

Round 7: Knit to first marker, remove marker, place 16 thumb sts on holder, remove second M, CO 2 sts to right needle, knit to end of rnd.

Knit every round on mitt until it measures 11.5cm (4½in) from thumb hole OR until mitt measures 3.5cm (1⅜in) shorter than desired mitt length.

MITT TIP

Next round: K15, PM, k26, PM, k11.

Next round (dec): [Knit to 3 sts before marker, ssk, k1, SM, k1, k2tog] twice, knit to end of rnd.

Next round: Knit.

Rep last 2 rounds until 36 sts rem.

Rep only the dec rnd until 16 sts rem.

Next round: Knit to first marker, cut yarn leaving a 22.5cm (9in) tail. Place the 8 sts between markers on one needle; place the other 8 sts on a second needle. Cast off using Kitchener st.

THUMB

(Same for both hands.)

Place the 16 thumb sts on two 2.75mm (US 2) needles. With third needle, pick up and knit 4–6 sts (depending on how wide you would like the thumbs to be). Knit all rounds until thumb measures 5cm (2in), or desired length, from picked-up sts.

Next round: [K2tog] to end of rnd (10 sts).

Next round: [K2tog] to end of rnd (5 sts).

Cut yarn leaving a 10cm (4in) tail. With tapestry needle, weave tail into all rem sts and pull to close. Weave in all tails.

LEFT ARM-WARMER

Work as for Right Arm-Warmer to start of Right Hand.

LEFT HAND

Round 1: Using 2.75mm (US 2) needles, k10, PM, k10, PM, knit to end. Complete left hand as for right hand until Mitt Tip.

MITT TIP

Next round: K11, PM, k26, PM, k15. Complete as for Right Hand.

FINGERLESS MITTS

Work right and left hands as for Full Mittens until hand measures 7.5cm (3in) and thumbs measure 2cm (⅞in) or just shorter than desired length. Finish hands and thumbs with the foll 4 rounds:

Next round: Purl.

Next round: [Yo, k2tog] to end of rnd.

Next round: Purl.

Using 2.25mm (US 1) needle, cast off.

Striped Mittens

These simple stripy mittens are the same front and back. A nubbly, tweedy yarn adds textural and visual interest to a traditional design. Designed by Katharine Hunt.

YARN

Debbie Bliss *Donegal Aran Tweed* (100% wool), approx. 50g/88m per ball
- 2 balls of Black 01 **(MC)**
- 1 ball of Natural 04 **(A)**

NEEDLES

Pair of 4.50mm (US 7) knitting needles
Pair of 4.00mm (US 6) knitting needles
Two stitch markers
Two small stitch holders (or safety pins)
Darning needle

TENSION
---

18 sts and 26 rows = 10cm (4in) square measured over St st, using 4.50mm (US 7) needles.

TO FIT	SKILL LEVEL
One size	Beginner

SPECIAL ABBREVIATIONS

See page 95 for information on: inc 1, m1l, m1r.

MITTENS (MAKE 2)

With 4.50mm (US 7) needles and MC, CO 41 sts and work in k1, p1 rib for 7.5cm (3in), ending with a WS row. Work 2 rows St st.

THUMB GUSSET

*Change to A.

Row 1 (RS): K20, PM, m1, k1, m1, PM, k20 (3 sts between markers) (43 sts).

Note: Advance markers on each row along with knitting.

Row 2: Purl.

Change to MC.

Row 3: Knit.

Row 4: Purl.**

Work in stripe pattern from * as set, to **, alt 2 rows in each colour. Do not break yarn between stripes.

Cont inc the gusset as on Row 1, having 2 sts more inside markers on next, then every foll fourth row, until 13 sts between markers (53 sts).

Work 3 rows straight in St st, ending with a WS row in MC.

Next row (RS): With A, knit to first marker, slip 13 gusset sts to a holder to be worked later, dropping markers, inc 1, work to end of row (41 sts).

Cont to work in St st stripes until hand measures 6.5cm (2½in) from top of gusset, ending with a WS row in MC.

SHAPE TOP

Break A and cont with MC in St st to top of mitt as follows:

Row 1 (RS): K1, skpo, k35, k2tog, k1 (39 sts).

Row 2 and all WS rows: Purl.

Row 3: K1, skpo, k33, k2tog, k1 (37 sts).

Row 5: K1, skpo, k31, k2tog, k1 (35 sts).

Change to 4.00mm (US 6) needles.

Row 7: K1, skpo, k12, k2tog, k1, skpo, k12, k2tog, k1 (31 sts).

Row 9: K1, skpo, k10, k2tog, k1, skpo, k10, k2tog, k1 (27 sts).

Row 11: K1, skpo, k8, k2tog, k1, skpo, k8, k2tog, k1 (23 sts).

Row 13: K1, skpo, k6, k2tog, k1, skpo, k6, k2tog, k1 (19 sts).

Row 14: Cast off purlwise.

MAKE THUMB

Slip 13 sts from holder to 4.00mm (US 6) needle. Join MC and cont to end of thumb:

Next row (RS): Inc 1, knit to last st, inc 1 (15 sts).

Work in St st for 7 rows.

SHAPE TIP

Row 1 (RS): [K1, k2tog] across row (10 sts).

Row 2: Purl.

Row 3: K2tog across row (5 sts).

Cut yarn, leaving end long enough to sew thumb seam.

Thread end through rem sts. Draw up and fasten securely.

FINISHING

Sew thumb seam. With RS facing, sew side and top seams, taking care to match stripes.

ZEBRA CROSSING

For neat edges and smooth seams, insert the needle as if to work the next st after completing the first st in every row. Before completing the st, give the working yarn a gentle pull to tighten up the edge, then cont across row.

Ribbon Wrist-Warmers

Satin ribbons add a pretty detail to these quick-knit fingerless gloves. For some extra sparkle or colour, stitch a few beads to the back of the hand. Designed by Sue Bradley.

YARN

RYC *Soft Tweed* (56% wool, 20% viscose, 14% polyamide, 10% silk), approx. 50g/80m per ball
  2 balls of Antique 02

NEEDLES

Pair of 5.00mm (US 8) knitting needles
Pair of 7.00mm (US 10½) knitting needles

RIBBON

3m (3¼yd) of satin ribbon,10–15mm (⅜–⅝in) wide

TENSION

13 sts and 18 rows = 10cm (4in) square measured over St st using 7.00mm (US 10½) needles.

TO FIT	SKILL LEVEL
One size	Beginner

WRIST-WARMERS (MAKE 2)

Using 5.00mm (US 8) needles, CO 28 sts.

Work in k1, p1 rib for 10 rows.

Change to 7.00mm (US 10½) needles and knit 2 rows.

Work 4 rows in St st.

Next row: Knit, wrapping yarn around needle (yrn) twice on every stitch of row.

Next row: Purl, dropping yrn.

With RS facing, work 4 rows in St st.

MAKE LACE HOLES

Next row: *K2, yo, k2tog; rep from * to end.

Next row: Purl.

Next row: *K1, yo, k2tog, k1; rep from * to end.

Next row: Purl.

Work 2 rows in St st.

Next row: Knit, wrapping yarn around needle (yrn) twice on every stitch of row.

Next row: Purl, dropping each yrn.

THUMB GUSSET (LEFT MITTEN)

Row 1: K11, inc in next st, k2, inc in next st, k13 (30 sts).

Row 2: Purl.

Row 3: K11, inc in next st, k4, inc in next st, k13 (32 sts).

Row 4: Purl.

Row 5: K11, inc in next st, k6, inc in next st, k13 (34 sts).

Row 6: Purl.

NB: For right mitten, work in reverse by beginning each RS row with k13 and end with k11.

THUMB (LEFT MITTEN)

Row 1: K21, turn and leave rem 13 sts on stitch holder.

(Right mitten k22, turn and leave rem 12 sts on stitch holder.)

Row 2: CO 2 sts, p10, turn and leave rem sts on stitch holder, CO 2 sts (12 sts).

Row 3: Knit.

Row 4: Purl.

Row 5: Knit.

Row 6: Purl.

Knit 2 rows.

Cast off.

With RS facing, knit across all of the sts on stitch holder (26 sts).

Next row: Purl.

Work 2 rows St st.

Next row: Knit, wrapping yarn around needle (yrn) twice on every stitch of row.

Next row: Purl, dropping yrn.

Work 2 rows in St st.

Knit 2 rows.

Cast off.

FINISHING

Sew in ends and lightly press pieces under a damp cloth.

With right sides together, sew up edges of mitten and thumb seams.

RIBBON DECORATION

Cut 6 x 30cm (12in) lengths of ribbon to thread through the dropped stitch rows, and 2 x 45cm (18in) lengths of ribbon to thread through the lace holes. Turn mitten inside out and neatly hand-stitch one end of the ribbon to the side seam. Now thread the ribbon into a large, blunt-ended darning needle, or safety pin, and use this to thread the ribbon in and out of the dropped stitches/lace holes. Stitch the other end of the ribbon carefully to the side seam.

NO STRINGS ATTACHED

If you want to lengthen the cuff, simply work a longer rib. To add a hint of whimsy, embellish with a patterned ribbon.

Lace Gloves

Lacy gloves with a touch of sparkle are perfect for eveningwear. A delicate diamanté button sits on the outside cuff to finish off the look. Designed by Judy Furlong.

YARN

Twilley's *Goldfingering* (80% viscose, 20% metallized polyester), approx. 50g/200m per ball

    2 balls of Ebony 31

NEEDLES

Pair of 3.00mm (US 2/3) knitting needles.

Two stitch markers

Two row markers

Sewing needle and thread

BUTTONS

Two buttons, 1cm (½in) in diameter

TENSION

28 sts and 38 rows = 10cm (4in) square measured over St st using 3.00mm (US 2/3) needles.

TO FIT

One size

SKILL LEVEL

Advanced

SPECIAL ABBREVIATIONS

See page 95 for information on: inc 1, sl1, yfwd.

BEAD STITCH (BS)

Multiple of 6 + 1 sts.

This is a traditional Shetland lace pattern, with every row knit.

Row 1: SM, k2, *yo, sl1, k2tog, psso, yo, k3; rep from * the number of times stated in the pattern (5 sts before next marker), yo, sl1, k2tog, psso, yo, k2, SM.

Row 2: SM, k1, k2tog, *yo, k1, yo, k2tog, k1, k2tog; rep from * the number of times stated in the pattern (4 sts before next marker), yo, k1, yo, k2tog, k1, SM.

Row 3: SM, k2tog, yo, *k3, yo, sl1, k2tog, psso, yo; rep from * the number of times stated in the pattern (5 sts before next marker), k3, yo, k2tog, SM.

Row 4: SM, k1, yo, k2tog, k1, *k2tog, yo, k1, yo, k2tog, k1; rep from * the number of times stated in the pattern (3 sts before next marker), k2tog, yo, k1, SM.

Lace row 4: K2, yo, k2tog, k1, k2tog, yo, k3.

Rep the last 4 rows twenty-three more times and the first row one more time, ending with WS facing.

Knit 3 rows, ending with RS facing.

Cast off 9 sts, one st now rem on RH needle.

Pick up and knit 53 sts (approx. 1 st every 2 rows) along nearest (LH) edge of peplum (54 sts).

THUMB GUSSET

Inc row (WS): K2, PM, k3, *inc 1, k5; rep from * three more times, PM, inc 1, k11, inc 1, k12 (31 sts between markers) (60 sts).

Row 1 (RS): K25, m1, k2, work BS Row 1; rep from * three times (working it four times in total), k2.

Row 2: K2, work BS Row 2; rep from * three times, purl to last 2 sts, k2.

Row 3: K28, work BS Row 3; rep from * three times, k2.

Row 4: K2, work BS Row 4; rep from * three times, purl to last 2 sts, k2.

Row 5: K25, m1, k3, work BS Row 1; rep from * three times, K2.

Row 6: As Row 2.

Row 7: K29, work BS Row 3; rep from * three times, k2.

Row 8 (mark both ends of this row): K2, SM, work BS Row 4; rep from

CHAIN STITCH LOOP

Secure a length of yarn to the edge of the glove. Insert the needle back in at the same point and draw up to make a small loop. Insert needle into this loop from underneath and reinsert from on top. Gently tighten up the first loop. Rep until chain is desired length to accommodate the button. Fasten to glove edge, forming a loop.

LEFT GLOVE

PEPLUM

CO 10 sts. Work 3 rows in garter stitch.

Lace row 1 (RS): K4, yo sl1, k2tog, psso, yo, k3.

Lace row 2: K2, k2tog, yo, k1, yo, k2tog, k3.

Lace row 3: K2, k2tog, yo, k3, yo, k2tog, k1.

* three times, SM, purl to last 2 sts, k2 (62 sts).

Row 9: K25, m1, k8, m1, k2, PM, work BS Row 1, rep from * once (working it twice in total), PM, k8.

Row 10: P8, work BS Row 2; rep from * once, purl to end of row.

Row 11: Knit to marker, work BS Row 3; rep from * once, k8.

Row 12: P8, work BS Row 4; rep from * once, purl to end of row.

Row 13: K25, m1, k10, m1, k2, work BS Row 1; rep from * once, k8.

Rows 14–16: Rep Rows 10–12.

Row 17: K25, m1, k12, m1, k2, work BS Row 1; rep from * once, k8.

Rows 18–20: Rep Rows 10–12 (68 sts).

Row 21: K25, m1, k14, m1, k2, work BS Row 1; rep from * once, k8.

Rows 22–24: Rep Rows 10–12, removing both markers on the last row (70 sts).

MAKE THUMB

Next row: K41, turn, CO 3 sts.

Next row: P19, turn, CO 3 sts (22 sts). Starting with a knit row, work 20 rows on these 22 sts.

SHAPE TOP

Next row: K1, *k2tog, k2; rep from * to last st, k1 (17 sts).

Next row: Purl.

Next row: K1, *k2tog; rep from * to end

of row (9 sts).
Break off yarn, thread through rem sts, draw up and fasten off.
Sew seam.

MAIN SECTION

Row 1: With RS facing, rejoin yarn, pick up and knit 5 sts at base of thumb, k10, yo, sl1, k2tog, psso, yo, knit to end of row (59 sts).

Row 2: P14, k1, k2tog, yo, k1, yo, k2tog, k1, p10, p2tog, purl to end of row (58 sts).

Row 3: K37, k2tog, yo, k3, yo, k2tog, knit to end of row.

Row 4: P14, k1, yo, k2tog, k1, k2tog, yo, k1, purl to end of row.

Row 5: K39, yo, sl1, k2tog, psso, yo, knit to end of row.

Row 6: P14, k1, k2tog, yo, k1, yo, K2tog, k1, purl to end of row.

Row 7: As Main Section Row 3.

Row 8: As Main Section Row 4.

Rep the last 4 rows.

DIVIDE FOR FOURTH FINGER

Next row: K39, yo, sl1, k2tog, psso, yo, k9, turn (7 sts rem unworked), CO 2 sts.

Next row: P9, k1, k2tog, yo, k1, yo, k2tog, k1, p30, turn (7 sts rem unworked), CO 2 sts.

Next row: K32, k2tog, yo, k3, yo, k2tog, k9, turn.

Next row: P9, k1, yo, k2tog, k1, K2tog, yo, k1, p32, turn.

FINGERS

FIRST FINGER

Next row: K32, turn, CO 2 sts.

Next row: P18, turn, CO 2 sts (20 sts). On these 20 sts only, work a further 22 rows in St st.

SHAPE TOP

Next row: K1, *k2tog, k2; rep from * to last 3 sts, k2tog, k1 (15 sts).

Next row: Purl.

Next row: K1, *k2tog; rep from * to end of row (8 sts).

Break off yarn, thread through rem sts, draw up and fasten off.
Sew seam.

SECOND FINGER

Row 1: With RS facing, pick up and knit 3 sts from base of first finger, k2, yo, sl1, k2tog, psso, yo, k2, turn, CO 2 sts.

Row 2: P2, k1, k2tog, yo, k1, yo, k2tog, k1, p1, p2tog, p7, turn, CO 2sts (20 sts).

Cont on these 20 sts as foll:

Row 3: K11, k2tog, yo, k3, yo, k2tog, k2.

Row 4: P2, k1, yo, k2tog, k1, k2tog, yo, k1, p11.

Row 5: K13, yo, sl1, k2tog, psso, yo, k4.

Row 6: P2, k1, k2tog, yo, k1, yo, k2tog, k1, p11.

Row 7: As Row 3.

Row 8: As Row 4.

Rep last 4 rows a further five times.

SHAPE TOP

Work as for first finger.

Break off yarn, thread through rem sts, draw up and fasten off.

Sew seam.

THIRD FINGER

Row 1: With RS facing, rejoin yarn, pick up and knit 3 sts from base of second finger, k9, turn.

Next row: P10, p2tog, p9, turn (20 sts).

On these 20 sts only, work a further 22 rows in St st.

SHAPE TOP

As for first finger.

Break off yarn, thread through rem sts, draw up and fasten off.

Sew seam.

FOURTH FINGER

Next row: With RS facing, rejoin yarn, pick up and knit 3 sts from base of third finger, knit to end of row (17 sts).

Starting with a purl row, work a further 17 rows in St st.

Shape top

Next row: K1, *k2tog, k2; rep from * to the end (13 sts).

Next row: Purl.

Next row: K1, *k2tog; rep from * to the end (7 sts).

Break off yarn, thread through rem sts, draw up and fasten off.

Sew side seam as far as the garter st edge (at the row markers).

RIGHT GLOVE

PEPLUM

Work as for Left Glove.

THUMB GUSSET

Inc row (WS): K12, inc 1, k11, inc 1, PM, k5, *inc 1, k5; rep from * three more times (60 sts).

Row 1 (RS): K2, PM, work BS Row 1; rep from * three times (working it four times in total), k2, m1, k25.

Row 2: K2, p26, work BS Row 2; rep from * three times, k2.

Row 3: K2, work BS Row 3; rep from * three times, k28.

Row 4: K2, p26, work BS Row 4; rep from * three times, k2.

Row 5: K2, work BS Row 1; rep from * three times, k3, m1, k25.

Row 6: K2, p27, work BS Row 2; rep from * three times, k2.

Row 7: K2, work BS Row 3; rep from * three times, k29.

Row 8 (mark both ends of this row): K2, p27, work BS Row 4; rep from * three times and removing markers, k2.

Row 9: K8, SM, work BS Row 1; rep from * once and ignoring references to markers, PM, k2, m1, k8, m1, k25 (64 sts).

Row 10: Purl to first marker, work BS Row 2; rep from * once, p8.

Row 11: K8, PM, work BS Row 3; rep from * once, knit to end.

Row 12: Purl to first marker, work BS Row 4; rep from * once, p8.

Row 13: K8, work BS row 1; rep from * once, k2, m1, k10, m1, knit to end.

Rows 14–16: Rep Rows 10–12 (66 sts).

Row 17: K8, work BS Row 1; rep from * once, k2, m1, k12, m1, knit to end.

Rows 18–20: Rep Rows 10–12 (68 sts).

Row 21: K8, work BS Row 1; rep from * once, k2, m1, k14, m1, knit to end.

Rows 22–24: Rep Rows 10–12, removing markers on last row (70 sts).

THUMB

Next row: K16, *yo, sl1, k2tog, psso, yo, k26, turn, CO 3 sts.

Next row: P19, turn, CO 3 sts (22 sts).

Starting with a knit row, work a further 20 rows in St st on these 22 sts.

SHAPE TOP

Next row: K1, *k2tog, k2; rep from * to last st, k1 (17 sts).

Next row: Purl.

Next row: K1, *k2tog; rep from * to end of row (9 sts).

Break off yarn, thread through rem sts, draw up and fasten off.
Sew side seam.

MAIN SECTION

Row 1: With RS facing, rejoin yarn, pick up and knit 5 sts at base of thumb, knit to end of row (59 sts).

Row 2: P26, p2tog, p9, k1, k2tog, yo, k1, yo, k2tog, k1, purl to end of row (58 sts).

Row 3: K14, k2tog, yo, k3, yo, k2tog, knit to end of row.

Row 4: P37, k1, yo, k2tog, k1, k2tog, yo, k1, purl to end of row.

Row 5: K16, yo, sl1, k2tog, psso, yo, knit to end of row.

Row 6: P37, k1, k2tog, yo, k1, yo, k2tog, k1, purl to end of row.

Row 7: As Main Section Row 3.

Row 8: As Main Section Row 4.

Rep the last 4 rows.

DIVIDE FOR FOURTH FINGER

Next row: K16, yo, sl1, k2tog, psso, yo, k32, turn (7 sts rem unworked), CO 2 sts.

Next row: P32, k1, k2tog, yo, k1, yo, k2tog, k1, p7, turn (7 sts rem unworked), CO 2 sts.

Next row: K9, k2tog, yo, k3, yo, k2tog, k32, turn.

Next row: P32, k1, yo, k2tog, k1, k2tog, yo, k1, p9, turn.

FINGERS

FIRST FINGER

Next row: K11, yo, sl1, k2tog, psso, yo, k18, turn, CO 2 sts.

Next row: P18, turn, CO 2 sts (20 sts). On these 20 sts only, work a further 22 rows in St st.

SHAPE TOP

Work as for Left Glove first finger.

SECOND FINGER

Row 1: With RS facing, rejoin yarn, pick up and knit 3 sts from base of first finger, k7, turn, CO 2 sts.

Row 2: P9, p2tog, p1, k1, k2tog, yo, k1, yo, k2tog, k1, turn, CO 2 sts (20 sts).

Cont on these 20 sts as foll:

Row 3: K2, k2tog, yo, k3, yo, k2tog, k11.

Row 4: P11, k1, yo, k2tog, k1, k2tog, yo, k1, p2.

Row 5: K4, yo, sl1, k2tog, psso, yo, k13.

Row 6: P11, k1, k2tog, yo, k1, yo, k2tog, k1, p2.

Row 7: As Row 3.

Row 8: As Row 4.

Rep the last 4 rows a further five times.

SHAPE TOP

As for Left Glove first finger.

THIRD FINGER

Work as for Left Glove third finger.

FOURTH FINGER

As for Left Glove fourth finger.

FINISHING

Darn in loose ends.

Spray lightly with water and allow to dry thoroughly.

Sew a chain stitch loop at wrist (where peplum attaches to glove).

Sew a button on edge of palm side of each glove to correspond with the loop – it is easier to do this with sewing thread rather than using the Goldfingering yarn.

SHAPE UP

- Work the last row of shaping for the thumb and fingers tightly or with a finer needle.
- For fingerless gloves, work 4 rows of the thumb and fingers, then cast off.

Fair Isle Warmers

Suited to the more advanced knitter, this adorable design made with an eye-catching palette is sure to capture your heart. Why not make them as a gift for that special loved-one? Designed by Gabrielle Carter.

YARN

Debbie Bliss *Cashmerino Chunky* (55% merino, 33% microfibre, 12% cashmere), approx. 50g/65m per ball

- 1 ball of Fuschia 05 **(A)**
- 1 ball of Magenta 07 **(B)**
- 1 ball of Lime 12 **(C)**
- 1 ball of Taupe 14 **(D)**

- 2 balls of Chocolate 15 **(E)**
- 1 ball of Slate 20 **(F)**
- 1 ball of Burnt Orange 16 **(G)**

NEEDLES

Five 4.50mm (US 7) double-pointed needles (dpns)

TENSION

18 sts and 23 rows = 10cm (4in) square measured over St st using 4.50mm (US 7) needles.

TO FIT

One size

SKILL LEVEL

Advanced

SPECIAL ABBREVIATIONS

See page 95 for information on: C2F.

NOTE: As the dimensions are given in cm rather than specific rounds, each new sequence begins with Round 1. Remember to twist the yarn in as the pattern moves: this will make for smaller floats, which is important when trying to fit the gloves correctly.

GLOVE (MAKE 2)
BODY

Using 4.50mm (US 7) needles, CO 36 sts using long-tail method. Arrange sts on four needles.

Round 1: *K1, p1; rep from * to end of round (C2F to secure bridge on first round).

Rep round until k1, p1 rib cuff measures 6cm (2¼in) – approx. 15 rounds.

At the beg of next round, change stitch to moss stitch as follows:

Round 1: *P1, k1; rep from * to end of round.

Round 2: *K1, p1; rep from * to end of round.

Rep these 2 rows for 5 rounds, ending on a Round 1 rep.

Change colour and complete 1 full round in purl. Work in purl from this point until end of Fair Isle pattern (with the exception of 2 rows in the middle).

The pattern is knitted in rounds from the inside as reverse stocking stitch.

Refer to chart for Fair Isle pattern and colour change directions. Cont with patt, including 2 rounds of continuous knit (stocking stitch) towards the top, until the glove body measures 19.5cm (7¾in) – approx. 50 rounds.

THUMB GAP

At the beg of the next round, work the sts straight, so working in rows rather than rounds. This results in a fork at the beginning/end of the rows.

Cont with the Fair Isle pattern and into the moss stitch on the hand throughout these rows; when knitting moss stitch, work the same sequence as before.

Work moss stitch for 3 rounds, until the thumb gap measures 4.5cm (1¾in).

To resume rounds, work the row until the penultimate st and then drop the final st on to a dpn and C2F. This should bridge the gap securely and allow you to work in rounds from this point.

UPPER HAND

Cont working in moss stitch for the upper hand until it measures 3cm (1¼in) from the top of the thumb gap; 27cm (11in) in total length.

FINGERS

Note: For all fingers you must knit half the sts before you work the sequence,

so the placement will be at the opposite end to the thumb gap.

LITTLE FINGER

Knit half round, k4, place foll 28 sts on holder leaving final 4 sts to work for little finger. Divide these 8 sts between three dpns.

On first round, work moss stitch until reaching the gap at the hand and C2F (using the 2 sts on either side of the hand gap).

Cont working little finger in moss stitch for further 2 rounds, moving into k1, p1 rib for the final 2 rounds. Cast off 8 sts. In order for the placement of the other fingers to be slightly higher than that of the little finger, 1 round must be completed before starting on second finger.

Reattach the yarn at the bridged finger gap to pull the gap together. Work 1 round in full.

THIRD FINGER

K4, place the foll 20 sts on hold leaving the final 4 sts to work for third finger. Divide these 8 sts between three dpns. On first round, work moss stitch until reaching the gap at the hand (and between the ring and little finger) and C2F. Cont working third finger in moss stitch for further 3 rounds, then move into k1, p1 rib for the final 2 rounds. Cast off 8 sts.

SECOND FINGER

Reattach yarn at the bridged finger gap, k5, place the foll 10 sts on hold leaving the final 5 sts to work for second finger. Divide these 10 sts between three dpns. On first round, work moss stitch until reaching the gap at the hand (and between the ring and middle finger) and C2F. Cont working second finger in moss stitch for further 3 rounds, then move into k1, p1 rib for the final 2 rounds. Cast off 10 sts.

FIRST FINGER

Reattach yarn at the bridged finger gap and make 2 sts through picking up the bar at the middle finger bridge, leaving 12 sts to divide between four needles. Divide these 12 sts between three dpns. On first round, work moss stitch until reaching the gap at the hand (and between the middle and index finger), C2F. Cont working first finger in moss stitch for further 4 rounds, then move into k1, p1 rib for the final 2 rounds. Cast off 12 sts.

FINISHING

Weave in all ends and reinforce.

A B C D E F G

☒ Knit stitch/ change of colour

☐ Reverse St st

Marshmallow Muff

This gorgeous, super-soft hand-warmer in luxurious mohair, which can be worn on its own or with a detachable cord that goes around the neck or through a jacket, is an ideal project for a quick fix of knitting. Designed by Sophie Britten.

YARN

Rowan *Romance* (36% acrylic, 27% nylon, 26% mohair, 8% polyester, 3% wool), approx. 50g/55m per ball
  2 balls of Glitter 90 **(A)**
  2 balls of Sparkle 95 **(B)**

NEEDLES

Pair of 7.00mm (US 10½/11) knitting needles
Two 4.00mm (US 6) circular needle
One tapestry needle

MATERIALS

A piece of stiff paper/cardboard for pompoms
Two small D-rings
Two 38mm (1½in) press studs

TENSION

12½ sts and 16 rows = 10cm (4in) square measured over St st using 7.00mm (US 10½/11) knitting needles and yarn doubled

TO FIT

One size

SKILL LEVEL

Beginner

MATTRESS STITCH

With WS facing, lay the fabric flat and fold in the two sides so that they are next to one another, RS now facing, with the stitches lined up row for row. Mattress stitch is worked by inserting the needle under the bar between the edge stitch and the one next to it. Using a tapestry needle, insert the needle under the bar of the first stitch on one side. Pull the yarn through and insert the needle under the parallel horizontal bar on the opposite side. Work back and forth until you reach the top. Do not fasten off: you can continue to work the seam at the top of the tube.

MUFF

Using A double, and 7.00mm (US 10½/11) needles, CO 46 sts.

Row 1: Knit.
Row 2: Purl.
Using B double:
Row 3: Knit.
Row 4: Purl.
Pick up A and cont to work straight in St st, alt colours A and B every other row, for 104 rows. Cast off, leaving a long tail for sewing up the muff.

POMPOMS (MAKE 4)

Cut two identical discs of cardboard measuring 4cm (1½in) in diameter. Cut a hole, 2cm (¾in) in diameter, in the centre of both discs. Cut off approximately 270cm (3yd) of colour A yarn.
Place the discs together. Pass the yarn through the centre of the hole, wrap the yarn around the outside of the discs making sure the rings are uniformly covered. Now cut the yarn at the edge of the ring by positioning the scissors in between the two pieces of cardboard. Take a piece of yarn 40cm (15in) long and, leaving one short tail and one long, wrap it very tightly in between the two discs, around the cut pieces, and tie a knot. Remove the cardboard discs and fluff out the pompom – you may need to trim it to make an even sphere. Trim off the short tail.

STRAP

Using two 4.00mm (US 6) dpns and colour B, CO 3 sts. Slide the sts to the other end of the needle, and carrying the yarn across the back, knit the next row.
Continue to knit and slide in this way until the strap measures 114cm (45in), then cast off. You may need to give the cord a tug as you go to pull it into a tube. Do not sew in ends.

INVISIBLE SHOULDER SEAM

Instead of aligning the stitches row by row, work horizontally and align stitch by stitch. Insert the needle behind the first stitch to the left of the seam you have just worked, under the CO row on the outer tube from right to left, and bring the needle through to the front of the work. Now insert the needle from right to left behind the corresponding stitch on the inner tube and then bring it through to the front of the work. Alt from outer to inner, work around the tube.

FINISHING

With RS of muff facing, sew up the long sides using mattress stitch; do not fasten off. Fold the muff in half, and you will now have a double-thickness tube.
With RS facing, sew up the end as you would an invisible shoulder seam. Sew in all ends.
Rearrange the muff so that the seam is centrally placed inside the muff.
Attach D-rings to either end of the muff. Using the tails, attach the press studs to either end of the strap.
Tie the two pompoms to each side of the strap.

Flip-Top Mitts

The multi-coloured yarn creates an amazing kaleidoscope effect on these cozy crocheted mittens. Try adjusting the size by adding more rows before shaping the top. Designed by Carol Meldrum.

YARN

Rowan *Tapestry* (70% wool, 30% soybean fibre), approx. 50g/120m per ball
  2 balls of Rainbow 171

NEEDLES

4.00mm (F/5) crochet hook

TENSION

18 sts and 9 rows = 4in (10cm) square measured over treble crochet using 4.00mm (F/5) hook.

TO FIT

One size

SKILL LEVEL

Advanced

SPECIAL ABBREVIATIONS

See page 95 for information on: trtog.

MITTEN (MAKE 2)

Make 41ch.

Row 1: 1dc into second ch from hook, 1dc into each chain to end.

Row 2: 1ch, 4dc, miss 4dc, *9tr into next dc, miss 3dc, 1dc into next dc, miss 3dc, rep from * ending 1dc in last dc, turn.

Row 3: 3ch, miss first dc, 4trtog over next 4tr, *4ch, 1dc into next tr (the centre of the 9tr), 3ch, 9trtog over [next 4tr, 1dc, 4tr], rep from * ending 5trtog over [last 4tr and 1ch], turn.

Row 4: 3ch, 4tr in top of 5trtog, *1dc in dc, miss 3ch, 9tr in top of 9trtog, rep from *, ending 5tr in top of 4trtog, turn.

Row 5: 3ch, miss first tr, *9trtog over [next 4tr, 1dc, 4tr], 3ch, 1dc in next tr (the centre of 9tr), 3ch, rep from * ending 1dc in top of tch, turn.

Row 6: 1ch, miss first dc, *miss 3ch, 9tr in top of 9trtog, miss 3ch, 1dc in dc, rep from *, working last dc in top first of 3ch, turn.

Rows 3–6 form pattern. Rep Rows 3–6 once more, then Rows 3–4 once again. Fasten off.

TOP

Make 35ch plus 2 tch.

Row 1: 1tr into third ch from hook, work 1tr into each ch to end, turn (35 sts).

Row 2: 2ch, 1tr into each tr of previous row, turn.

Rep Row 2 five times.

SHAPE TOP

Next row: 2ch, 2trtog as foll: (*yrh and insert into next st, yrh and draw through, yrh and under first 2 loops on hook; rep from * once more, yrh and under all 3 loops on hook), 13tr, 2trtog, 1tr, 2trtog, 12tr, 2trtog, 1tr, turn (31 sts).

Next row: 2ch, 2trtog, 11tr, 2trtog, 1tr, 2trtog, 10tr, 2trtog, 1tr, turn (27 sts).

Next row: 2ch, 2trtog, 9tr, 2trtog, 1tr, 2trtog, 8tr, 2trtog, 1tr, turn (23 sts).

Next row: 2ch, 2trtog, 7tr, 2trtog, 1tr, 2trtog, 6tr, 2trtog, 1tr, turn (19 sts).

Fasten off.

THUMB

Make 4ch, ss into first ch to form a ring.

Round 1: 2ch, 9tr into ring, ss into top of ch at beg of round.

Rounds 2–5: 2ch, 1tr into each tr of prev round, join with ss into top of ch at beg of round.

Round 6: 1ch, 1dc into next 3tr, 2tr into next tr, 1tr, 2tr into next tr, 1dc into next 3tr, ss into top of 1ch at beg of round (11 sts).

Round 7: 1ch, 1dc into next 3 sts, work 2htr into next st, 2tr into next st, 1tr, 2tr into next st, 2htr into next st, 1dc into next 3 sts, ss into top of 1ch at beg of round (15 sts).

Round 8: 1ch, 1dc into next 5 sts, work 2htr into next st, 2tr into next st, 1tr, 2tr into next st, 2htr into next st, 1dc into next 5 sts, ss into top of 1ch at beg of round (19 sts).

Round 9: 1ch, 1dc into next 7 sts, work 2htr into next st, 2tr into next st, 1tr, 2tr into next st, 2htr into next st, 1dc into next 7 sts, ss into top of 1ch at beg of round (23 sts).

Break off yarn.

FINISHING

Sew in all loose ends, block and press fabric.

Place a marker at centre point of both mitten top and base. Pin mitten top to the inside of mitten base along Row 10. Using backstitch, sew into position up to the centre point marker. Fold mitten top in half and stitch top and sides together. Fold mitten base in half, stitch up to Row 4, then stitch together Rows 10 upwards – this will leave a gap for your thumb. Pin thumb in position and stitch in place.

When stitching top flap in position, remember that for the left hand, stitch to the right-hand side of the base; for the right hand, stitch to the left of the base. This will ensure that both mittens flip in the same direction.

Cable Mittens

These warm and cosy mittens are knitted in a smart Donegal tweed and have an easy-to-work bobbly cable pattern running up the back of the hand. Designed by Katharine Hunt.

YARN

Debbie Bliss *Donegal Aran Tweed* (100% wool), approx. 50g/88m per ball
   2 balls of Purple 07

NEEDLES

Pair of 4.50mm (US 7) knitting needles
Pair of 4.00mm (US 6) knitting needles
One cable needle

EXTRAS

Two stitch markers
Two small stitch holders
One darning needle

TENSION

18 sts and 24 rows = 10cm (4in) square measured over St st using 4.50mm (US 7) needles.

TO FIT

One size

SKILL LEVEL

Intermediate

SPECIAL ABBREVIATIONS

See page 95 for information on: FC (front cross), BC (back cross), MK (make knot), and CP (bobbly cable pattern).

BOBBLY CABLE PATTERN

Panel worked over 15 sts.

Rows 1, 3, 5, 7 (WS): K5, p5, k5.

Row 2: P5, k2, MK, k2, p5.

Row 4: P5, MK, k3, MK, k5.

Row 6: P5, k2, MK, k2, p5.

Row 8: P4, BC, p1, FC, p4.

Row 9: K4, p2, k1, p1, k1, p2, k4.

Row 10: P3, BC, k1, p1, k1, FC, p3.

Row 11: K3, p3, k1, p1, k1, p3, k3.

Row 12: P2, BC, [p1, k1] twice, p1, FC, p2.

Row 13: K2, p2, [k1, p1] three times, k1, p2, k2.

Row 14: P2, k3, [p1, k1] twice, p1, k3, p2.

Rows 15, 17, 19: Rep Rows 13, 11 and 9.

Row 16: P2, FC, [p1, k1] twice, p1, BC, p2.

Row 18: P3, FC, k1, p1, k1, BC, p3.

Row 20: P4, FC, p1, BC, p4.

Rep Rows 1–20 twice more, then Rows 1–7 once.

This completes Bobbly Cable Pattern panel.

In subsequent rows, work these sts with background in reverse St st to end of mitten.

MITTENS

RIGHT MITTEN

With 4.50mm (US 7) needles, CO 41 sts.

Work 3 rows in k1, p1 rib, ending with RS row.

Next row (WS): Rib 23 sts, work Row 1 of Bobbly Cable Pattern (CP) over next 15 sts, p1, k1, p1.

Cont working rib and CP as set, until end of the first cable rep – cuff measures approx. 9cm (3½in), ending with RS row. Rib cuff is now complete. Cont in CP, working background in reverse St st throughout.

Next row (WS): K23, CP15, k3.

Work 2 more rows as set.

THUMB GUSSET

Row 1 (RS): P3, CP15, p2, PM, m1, p1, m1, PM, p20 (3 sts between markers) (43 sts).

NOTE: Advance markers on each row along with knitting.

Row 2: Knit to the last 18 sts, CP15, k3.

Row 3: P3, CP15, purl to end.

Row 4: As Row 2.

Keeping CP as set, cont inc gusset as on Row 1, having 2 sts more inside

markers on next, then every foll fourth row to 13 sts between markers (53 sts). Work 3 rows even, ending with WS row.

Next row (RS): Work to first marker. Slip 13 gusset sts on to st holders to be worked later, dropping markers. Inc 1 st and work to end of row (41 sts).

Cont to work in patt as set until hand measures 6.5cm (2½in) from top of gusset, ending with Row 1 of CP.

SHAPE TOP

Row 1 (RS): P1, p2tog, CP15, p20, p2tog tbl, p1 (39 sts).

Row 2 and all WS rows: Work even.

Row 3: P1, p2tog, CP14, p19, p2tog tbl, p1 (37 sts).

Row 5: P1, p2tog, CP13, p2tog tbl, p1, p2tog, p13, p2tog tbl, p1 (33 sts).

Change to 4.00mm (US 6) needles.

Row 7: P1, p2tog, p11, p2tog tbl, p1, p2tog, p11, p2tog tbl, p1 (29 sts).

Rows 8 and 10: Knit.

Row 9: P1, p2tog, p9, p2tog tbl, p1, p2tog, p9, p2tog tbl, p1 (25 sts).

Row 11: P1, p2tog, p7, p2tog tbl, p1, p2tog, p7, p2tog tbl, p1 (21 sts).

Row 12: Cast off knitwise.

THUMB

Slip 13 sts from holders to 4.00mm (US 6) needle.

RS: Join yarn and purl 1 row, inc 1 st at beg and end of row (15 sts).

Work in reverse St st for 7 rows.

SHAPE TOP

Row 1: [P1, p2tog] across row (10 sts).

Row 2: Knit.

Row 3: P2tog across row (5 sts).

Cut yarn, leaving end long enough to sew thumb seam.

Thread yarn through remaining sts. Draw up and fasten securely.

LEFT MITTEN

Cast on 41 sts and work 3 rows in k1, p1 rib, ending with RS row.

Next row (WS): Rib 3 sts, work first row of CP over the next 15 sts, rib 23. Cont working rib and CP as set, until end of the first cable rep and end of ribbed cuff as on Right Mitten, ending with RS row.

Next row (WS): K3, CP15, k23. Work 2 more rows as set.

THUMB GUSSET

Row 1 (RS): P20, PM, m1, p1, m1, PM, p2, CP15, p3 (3 sts between markers) (43 sts).

Row 2: K3, CP15, knit to end.

Row 3: P25, CP15, p3.

Row 4: As Row 2.

Keeping CP as set, cont inc gusset as on Right Mitten to 13 sts between markers (53 sts).

Work 3 rows even, ending with Row 1 of CP.

Next row (RS): Work to first marker. Slip 13 gusset sts on to a holder to be worked later, dropping markers. Inc 1 st and work to end of row (41 sts).

Cont to work in CP as set until hand measures 6.5cm (2½in) from top of gusset, ending with WS row.

SHAPE TOP

Row 1 (RS): P1, p2tog, p20, CP15, p2tog tbl, p1 (39 sts).

Row 2 and all WS rows: Work even.

Row 3: P1, p2tog, p19, CP14, p2tog tbl, p1 (37 sts).

Row 5: P1, p2tog, p13, p2tog tbl, p1, p2tog, CP13, p2tog tbl, p1 (33 sts).

Change to 4.00mm (US 6) needles.

Row 7: P1, p2tog, p11, p2tog tbl, p1, p2tog, p11, p2tog tbl, p1 (29 sts).

Row 9: P1, p2tog, p9, p2tog tbl, p1, p2tog, p9, p2tog tbl, p1 (25 sts).

Row 11: P1, p2tog, p7, p2tog tbl, p1, p2tog, p7, p2tog tbl, p1 (21 sts).

Row 12: Cast off knitwise.

THUMB

Finish thumb as on Right Mitten.

FINISHING

Sew thumb seams. Working with RS facing, sew side and top seams.

Accordion Gloves

Keep your hands and arms snug in these unusual accordion gloves, knitted in a soft silk and wool blend. They are worked in the round, so there are no seams to sew at the end! Designed by Gryphon Perkins.

YARN

Noro *Silk Garden* (45% silk, 45% kid mohair, 10% lambswool), approx. 50g/120m per ball

   3 balls of Colour 84

NEEDLES

Four 4.00mm (US 6) double-pointed needles (dpns)
Six 4.50mm (US 7) double-pointed needles (dpns)
Stitch holder

TENSION

18 sts and 24 rows = 10cm (4in) square measured over St st using 4.50mm (US 7) needles.

TO FIT

One size

SKILL LEVEL

Intermediate

RIGHT GLOVE

ACCORDION CUFF

Using 4.00mm (US 6) dpns, CO 42 sts.
Distribute sts evenly over three dpns and
work k1, p1 rib in the round until work
measures 3cm (1¼in). Change to
4.50mm (US 7) dpns and inc as follows:

Round 1: *K1, m1, k6; rep from * to
end.

Round 2 (and all even rounds): Knit.

Round 3: *K1, m1, k7; rep from * to
end.

Round 5: *K1, m1, k8; rep from * to
end.

Cont to inc in this manner until there are
22 sts on each needle.

Round 12: Purl.

Now dec as follows:

Round 13: *Ssk, k11; rep from * to
end.

Round 14 (and all even rounds):
Knit.

Round 15: *Ssk, k10; rep from * to
end.

Round 17: *Ssk, k9; rep from * to end.

Cont to dec in this manner until there
are 12 sts on each needle.

After final dec round, begin to inc again
immediately, as before, until there are
22 sts on each needle. Purl one round.
Dec again as before, until there are 10
sts on each needle.

Begin to inc once more to 20 sts on

each needle, purl 1 round, then dec
again until there are 8 sts on each
needle.

Change to 4.00mm (US 6) needles and
work k1, p1 rib for 4cm (1½in).

THUMB GUSSET

Change to 4.50mm (US 7) needles.

Round 1: K2, m1, k3, m1, k2, m1, k3,
m1, k2, m1, k3, m1, k3, m1, k2, m1,
k3, m1, k1 (33 sts).

Round 2: Knit.

Round 3: K2, m1, k1, m1, knit to end.
Knit 2 rounds.

Round 6: K2, m1, k3, m1, knit to end.
Knit 2 rounds.

Round 9: K2, m1, k5, m1, knit to end.
Knit 2 rounds.

Cont in this manner until thumb gusset
has 9 sts, then knit 2 more rounds.

Next round: K2, put 9 sts on holder,
CO 4 sts, knit to end.

Knit 1 round.

THUMB FOURCHETTE

Next round: K1, ssk, k2, k2tog, knit to
end.

Knit 1 round.

Next round: K1, ssk, k2tog, knit to
end.

Knit evenly to 5cm (2in) from thumb
fourchette.

FINGERS

LITTLE FINGER

K13. On a new needle and joining a
new yarn (do not break the old yarn),
k6, CO 3 sts. Leaving the rest of the
hand sts on two dpns (or a holder),
distribute these sts over three dpns and
knit in the round, trying the glove on
until the finger is 1cm (½in) from the
desired length. Knit the last 2 sts on
each needle together until there are
5 sts remaining. Pull yarn through all sts
and break.

THIRD FINGER

Using the yarn from the hand, pick up
3 sts from those CO for the little finger
fourchette.

Knit 2 rounds, ending 3 sts before the
little finger. Join new yarn, k9, CO 3 sts.
Distribute these sts over three dpns and
knit in the round, stopping 1cm (½in)
from the desired length, as with the little
finger. Knit last 2 sts on each needle tog
until 6 sts rem. Pull yarn through all sts
and break.

SECOND FINGER

Put 10 sts on a holder for the first
finger, leaving 4 sts on either side of the
third finger. Using the yarn from the
hand, pick up 3 sts from the third finger
fourchette, k4, CO 2 sts, k4. Distribute
sts over three dpns and work as for third
finger.

FIRST FINGER

Joining new yarn, pick up 2 sts from
second finger fourchette, k10. Distribute
sts over three dpns and work as for third
and second fingers.

THUMB

Joining new yarn, pick up sts from holder
and from fourchette (11 sts). Distribute
sts over three dpns and work as for
third, second, and first fingers.

LEFT GLOVE

Work as right glove, with the foll
exception to the thumb gusset – make
Round 3 as follows:

Round 3: Knit to last 3 sts, m1, k1,
m1, k2.

Knit 2 rounds.

Round 6: Knit to last 5 sts, m1, k3, m1,
k2.

Knit 2 rounds.

Round 9: Knit to last 7 sts, m1, k5,
m1, k2.

Knit 2 rounds.

Cont in this manner until the thumb
gusset has 9 sts, then knit 2 more
rounds.

Next round: Knit to last 9 sts, put on
holder, CO 4 sts, k2.

Knit 1 round.

DO THE STRAND

When joining a new yarn, strand the
two yarns together for 1 round to
soften the colour transition, unless
the new colour is very close to that
of the yarn just ending. Do not do
this when bringing in a new yarn at
the base of the little and third
fingers, as the old yarn needs to
remain where it is.

Bow Belles Mittens

These classic mittens, made in soft wool and cotton are made in one piece and adorned with a contrasting whisper-soft ribbon. Designed by Sophie Britten.

YARN

Rowan *Wool Cotton* (50% merino/50% cotton), approx 50g/113m per ball
  1 ball of Antique 900 **(MC)**
Rowan *Kidsilk Haze* (70% kid mohair/30% silk), approx 25g/210m per ball
  2 balls of Candy Girl 606 **(A)**

NEEDLES

Pair of 4.00mm (US 6) needles
One 2.50mm (C/2) crochet hook
One 4.00mm (US 6) circular needle
Tapestry needle

TENSION

Mittens: 23 sts and 29 rows = 10cm (4in) square measured over St st using 4.00mm (US 6) knitting needles.
Ribbon: 26 sts and 28 rows = 10cm (4in) square measured over St st using 4.00mm (US 6) knitting needles.

TO FIT

One size

SKILL LEVEL

Intermediate

SPECIAL ABBREVIATIONS

See page 95 for information on: m1l, m1r

MITTEN (MAKE 2)

CUFF

Using MC and 4.00mm (US 6) needles,
CO 39 sts using thumb method.
Starting with a purl row, work 17 rows
in St st, ending with a purl row.

PALM

Work all WS rows in purl.

Next knit row: K3, m1l, k16, m1l, k1,
m1r, k16, m1r, k3 (43 sts).

Next knit row: K3, m1l, k17, m1l, k3,
m1r, k17, m1r, k3 (47 sts).

Next knit row: K21, m1l, k5, m1r, k21
(49 sts).

Next knit row: K21, m1l, k7, m1r, k21
(51 sts).

Next knit row: K21, m1l, k9, m1r, k21
(53 sts).

Next knit row: K21, m1l, k11, m1r,
k21 (55 sts).

Work 1 row in purl.

THUMB

Row 1: K34, slip rem sts on to circular
needle.

Row 2: P13, slip rem sts on to circular
needle.

Rows 3–12: Work straight in St st.

Next row: K1, *k2tog, k1; rep from * to
end.

Next row: Purl.

Next row: [K2tog, k1] three times.

Slip all sts on to a crochet hook, wrap the yarn round the hook and draw through all sts on hook. With RS facing, close thumb by working 1 row of slip stitch down side of thumb, inserting the hook into the RH strand of the edge stitch nearest you and into the LH strand of the back edge. Keep remaining loop on hook – this will be picked up in the next row.

With RS facing, slip the first 21 sts on the straight needle, slip loop from crochet hook on to needle and knit across rest of row (43 sts).

Next row: Purl.

Work 16 rows straight in St st.

Work all WS rows in purl.

Next knit row: K1, k2tog, k16, k2tog, k1, k2tog, k16, k2tog, k1 (39 sts).

Next knit row: K1, k2tog, k14, k2tog, k1, k2tog, k14, k2tog, k1 (35 sts).

Next knit row: K1, k2tog, k12, k2tog, k1, k2tog, k12, k2tog, k1 (31 sts).

Next knit row: K1, *k2tog, k1; rep from * to end (21 sts).

Next knit row: [K1, k2tog] three times, k3, [k2tog, k1] three times (15 sts).

Next row: P6, p2tog, slip last st back on to left needle, fold work in half with RS facing, so both needles are facing the same way with 7 sts on each needle.

Insert the tip of a third needle (you can use the circular needle here) into the first st of one needle, then into the first st of the other needle; knit the first st from each needle together. Pass the previous st over this st to bind off, rep until 1 loop remains on right needle, transfer loop to crochet hook. Slip stitch down the side seam, inserting the hook into the RH strand of the edge st nearest you and into the LH strand of the back edge. Do not fasten off.

CUFF EDGE

Still using the crochet hook, work 1 round of dc into each st around bottom of cuff, slip stitch into first st. Fasten off.

RIBBONS (MAKE 2)

Using A and 4.00mm (US 6) needles, cast on 3 sts.

Working in St st, inc 1 st at beg of next and each knit row until there are 12 sts. Work straight in St st until ribbon measures 50cm (20in).

K2tog at beg of next and each knit row until 3 sts rem.

Cast off rem 3 sts on purl row.

FINISHING

Sew in all ends. Gently press all items. Wrap the ribbon around each mitten and tie in a bow, then arrange and sew ribbon in place on inner wrist.

THE END
If you don't want to finish the mitten in crochet, simply cut the yarn leaving a long tail and thread it through all the remaining loops, drawing them closed. Now sew down the side of the thumb/mitten making an invisible seam. After you have sewn up the thumb, and slipped the first 21 sts back on your needle, pick up a st where the thumb meets the palm in the following row. These mittens are also finished with a round of crochet around the bottom, which will stop the cuff from rolling up and into the bow.

Peacock Flip Mittens

An unusual peacock scallop pattern accompanies these mitts to create an eye-catching display. This is a more challenging project, guaranteed to yield impressive results. Designed by Gabrielle Carter.

YARN

RYC *Alpaca Soft* (50% alpaca/50% cotton), approx 50g/55m per ball
  3 balls of Whitewash 266

NEEDLES

Five 4.50mm (US 7) double pointed needles (dpns)

BUTTON

Decorative button

TENSION

20 sts and 22 rows = 10cm (4in) square measured over k1, p1 rib using 4.50mm (US 7) needles.

TO FIT

One size

SKILL LEVEL

Intermediate

SPECIAL ABBREVIATIONS

See page 95 for information on: C2F.

MITTENS
BODY
Using 4.50mm (US 7) needles, CO
28 sts using long-tail method.

Round 1: *K1, p1; rep from * to end of
round (C2F to secure bridge on this first
round).

Rep this round until the rib measures
around 13cm (5¼in) – approx.
29 rounds.

Cont working in k1, p1 rib throughout
gusset inc.

THUMB GUSSET
Next round: Rib 14, PM, m1, k1, m1,
PM (2 sts in), rib to end of round
(30 sts).

Rib 2 rounds.

Inc round: Rib to marker, SM, m1, rib
to marker, m1, SM, rib to end of round
(32 sts).

Rib 2 rounds even.

Rep inc round.

Rib 3 rounds even.

Rep the prev 4 rounds twice more
(38 sts).

NB: The 10 stitches between the
markers are used for the thumb gusset.

Next round: Rib to gusset, place
10 sts between markers on hold, rib to
end of round (28 sts).

Next round: Work to 1 st before gap
created by the thumb gusset, C2F, rib to
the end of round.

Knit 1 round, creating a purl ridge on
the right side of the mitten, and inc
11 sts evenly throughout round (39 sts).

UPPER HAND
Row 1: *Sppo, p9, p2tog; rep from * to
end of round.

Rows 2 and 4: Purl.

Row 3: *Sppo, p7, p2tog; rep from * to
end of round.

Row 5: *Sppo, yrn, [p1, yrn] five times,
p2tog; rep from * to end of round.

Row 6: Knit (creating raised ridge).

These 6 rows form scallop pattern;
13 sts for each of three scallops.

Rep these 6 rows for 5cm (2in) –
approx. 2 reps (39 sts).

FINGERS
**NOTE: For all fingers you must knit
half the sts on the needle before you
work the sequence, so that the
placement is at the opposite end to
the thumb gap.**

LITTLE FINGER
Knit half round, k5, place foll 30 sts on
hold leaving final 4 sts to work for little
finger. Divide these 9 sts between three
dpns.

Work in reverse St st (purl all sts) for
4 rounds; on first round C2F at hand
gap (using 2 sts on either side of hand
gap) to bridge.

Cast off 9 sts.

Reattach the yarn at the bridged finger
gap, pulling the gap together. In order
for the placement of the other fingers to
be slightly higher than that of the little
finger, work 1 round before starting on
the third finger.

THIRD FINGER
Reattach yarn at bridged finger gap, K5,
place foll 20 sts on hold leaving final 5
sts to work for third finger. Divide these
10 sts between three dpns.

Work in reverse St st for 4 rounds; on
first round C2F at hand and finger gap
(using 2 sts on either side of gap) to
bridge.

Cast off 10 sts.

SECOND FINGER
Reattach yarn at bridged finger gap, K5,
place foll 10 sts on hold leaving final 5
sts to work for second finger. Divide
these 10 sts between three dpns.

Work in reverse St st for 4 rounds; on
first round C2F at hand and finger gap
(using 2 sts on either side of gap) to
bridge.

Cast off 10 sts.

FIRST FINGER
Reattach yarn at bridged finger gap, k5,
place foll 10 sts on hold leaving final
5 sts to work for first finger. Divide these
10 sts between three dpns.

Work in reverse St st for 4 rounds; on

first round C2F at hand and finger gap (using 2 sts on either side of gap) to bridge.
Cast off 10 sts.

THUMB

Divide the stitches on hold between three dpns and rejoin yarn at gusset point.

Work in k1, p1 rib rounds until the thumb measures 4.5cm (1¾in).

CLOSE TOP OF THUMB

Next round: P2tog; rep to end (5 sts).

Thread a spare piece of yarn through these 5 sts and draw tog.

Weave in all ends and reinforce any gaps that may have formed between the fingers.

Turn mitt to right side.

MITTEN FLAP

Pick up 19 sts across back of hand at 1cm (⅜in) above lowest purl ridge (or wherever comfortable). At the end of this pick-up, CO 19 sts.

Divide these 38 sts between four dpns. Work 2 rounds in k1, p1 rib.

On last st of second round, m1 (39 sts). Divide these 39 sts equally across the needles.

Work two complete scallop sequences in full, finishing with a raised round.

Work 5 rounds in reverse St st.

BEGIN DEC FOR CAP

Round 1: *P1, p2tog; rep from * to end of round (26 sts).

Round 2: *P2tog; rep from * to end of round (13 sts).

Round 3: P1 *p2 tog; rep from * to end of round.

Rep this 2-row sequence until there are 6 sts rem.

Thread a spare piece of yarn through these 6 sts and draw tog.

Weave in all ends

Turn cap to right side.

FINISHING

Either crochet or plait a small loop around 3cm (1¼in) long and attach to crown of flap. Measuring on hand, stitch a button at the correct point on back of hand to secure flap when not in use. Alternatively, knit in a knitted button loop by tying in a double strand and backstitching around the loop.

Clock Wrist-Warmers

The frilled cuff on these stylish fingerless gloves takes clock-watching to a new level. It could also be knitted in a contrasting colour for an edgy look. Designed by Sue Bradley.

YARN

Rowan *Pure Wool DK* (100% merino wool), approx. 50g/122m per ball
  2 balls of Black 04 **(A)**
  1 ball of Snow 12 **(B)**
Twilley's *Goldfingering* (80% viscose, 20% metallized polyester), approx. 25g/200m per ball
  1 ball of Pink Multi 14 **(C)**

NEEDLES

Pair of 3.25mm (US 3) knitting needles
Pair of 4.00mm (US 6) knitting needles

SEQUINS

150 small silver sequins

TENSION

22 sts and 30 rows = 10cm (4in) square measured over St st using 4.00mm (US 6) needles.

TO FIT

One size

SKILL LEVEL

Advanced

RIGHT GLOVE

Using 3.25mm (US 3) needles and A, CO 48 sts and work 16 rows of k1, p1 rib.

Change to 4.00mm (US 6) needles and work 6 rows of St st in A.
Row 23 (RS facing): K9 in A, k5 in C, k34 in A (this places position of chart).

Rows 24–26: Work in St st from chart.

Row 27: K4 in A, patt the 15 sts of chart, k5 in A, in A inc in next st, k1, inc in next st, k21 (50 sts).

Rows 28–30: Work in St st and cont to follow the chart over the 15 sts.

Row 31: In colours as set, k24, inc in next st, k3, inc in next st, k21 (52 sts).

Rows 32–43: Work from chart, and on every fourth row inc first at each side of thumb for gusset as set (58 sts).

Rows 44–46: Work in St st.

THUMB

Row 47 (RS facing): In A, k38, turn and leave rem sts unworked on stitch holder, CO 2 sts.

Row 48: P16, turn and leave rem sts on stitch holder, CO 2 sts.

Rows 49–55 (RS facing): Work in St st for 7 rows, cast off knitwise.

With RH needle, pick up and knit 2 sts on each side at base of thumb, knit across the sts on first stitch holder.

Next row: Purl across sts, then purl across sts on second stitch holder (48 sts).

Starting with a knit row, work in St st for 8 rows.

FINGERS

FIRST FINGER

Next row (RS facing): K31, turn and leave sts unworked on a stitch holder, CO 1 st.

Next row: P15, turn and leave rem sts on a stitch holder, CO 1 st.

Starting with a knit row, work in St st for 7 rows, cast off knitwise.

SECOND FINGER

With RH needle, pick up and knit 2 sts at base of first finger, knit across 6 sts on first stitch holder, turn and CO 1 st.

Next row: Purl across these 9 sts and then 6 sts from the second stitch holder, turn and CO 1 st (16 sts).

Leave sts unworked on stitch holders.

Starting with a knit row, work in St st for 7 rows, cast off knitwise.

THIRD FINGER

Work as for second finger.

LITTLE FINGER

With RH needle, knit up the 2 sts at base of third finger, knit across rem 5 sts from first stitch holder.

Next row: Purl across these 7 sts and then purl rem 5 sts from second stitch holder (12 sts). Starting with a knit row, work in St st for 7 rows, cast off knitwise.

LEFT GLOVE

Rows 1–22: Work as Right Glove.
Row 23: K34 in A, k5 in C, k9 in A (this places position of chart).
Rows 24–26: Work in St st from chart.
Row 27: In A, k21, inc in next st, k1, inc in next st, k5, patt the 15 sts of chart, k4 (50 sts).
Rows 28–30: Work in St st and cont to follow the chart over the 15 sts.
Row 31: In A, k21, inc in next st, k3, inc in next st, k24.
Rows 32–43: Work from chart, and on every fourth row inc 1 st at each side of thumb for gusset as set (58 sts).
Rows 44–46: Work in St st.

THUMB

Row 47 (RS facing): In A, k34, turn and leave sts unworked on a stitch holder, CO 2 sts. Finish thumb and fingers as for Right Glove.

BELL FRILLING ON CUFF (OPTIONAL)

Using 3.25mm (US 3) needles and A, and with RS facing, pick up and knit 40 sts evenly along the CO edge of rib.

Purl 1 row.
Row 1 (RS facing): K1, *p3, k1; rep from * to last 3 sts, p3.
Row 2: *K3, p1, rep from * to last 4 sts, k3, p1.
Row 3: K1, *p3, yon, k1, yon; rep from * to last 3 sts, p3.
Row 4: *K3, p3; rep from * to last 4 sts, k3, p1.
Row 5: K1, *p3, yon, k3, yon; rep from * to last 3 sts, p3.
Row 6: *K3, p5; rep from * to last 4 sts, k3, p1.
Row 7: K1, *p3, yon, k5, yon; rep from * to last 3 sts, p3.
Row 8: *K3, p7; rep from * to last 4 sts, k3, p1.
Row 9: K1, *p3, yon, k7, yon; rep from * to last 3 sts, p3.
Row 10: * K3, p9; rep from * to last 4 sts, k3, p1.
Row 11: K1, *p3, yon, k9, yon; rep from * to last 3 sts, p3.
Row 12: * K3, p11; rep from * to last 4 sts, k3, p1.
Cast off knit sts knitwise and purl sts purlwise.

FINISHING

Sew in ends; press carefully. Join edges of thumb and fingers and edge of glove together. Decorate ends of fingers and thumb with silver sequins.

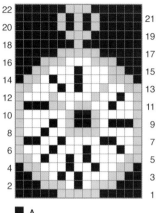

■ A
□ B
▨ C

ALL IN THE DETAIL

The wrist-warmers may be knitted without the motif and then decorated with sequins or beads for an entirely new look.

Firecracker Mitts

Expect fireworks when you wear these cracking mitts. The stylish pattern and super-soft wool yarn make them just right for city wear. Designed by Carol Meldrum.

YARN

Rowan *Scottish Tweed 4-ply* (100% wool), approx. 25g/110m per ball
  1 ball of Claret 13 **(A)**
  1 ball of Brilliant Pink 10 **(B)**
Rowan *Kidsilk Haze* (70% kid mohair, 30% silk), approx. 25g/210m per ball
  1 ball of Marmalade 596 **(C)**
  1 ball of Blueberry 600 **(D)**

NEEDLES

Pair of 4.00mm (US 6) knitting needles
Pair of 3.25mm (US 3) knitting needles

TENSION

22 sts and 30 rows = 10cm (4in) square measured over St st using 4.00mm (US 6) needles and *Kidsilk Haze* and *Scottish Tweed* together.

TO FIT	SKILL LEVEL
One size	Intermediate/ advanced

MITTS (MAKE 2)

Using 3.25mm (US 3) needles and
yarns A and C tog, CO 49 sts.

Row 1: K1, *p1, k1; rep from * to end.
Change to yarns B and D tog.

Row 2: P1, *k1, p1; rep from * to end.

Row 3: K1, *p1, k1; rep from * to end.
Rep Rows 2–3 eight more times.
Change to 4.00mm (US 6) needles.

Row 19: Knit to end, inc 1 st at end of
row (50 sts).

Row 20: Purl.

Row 21: K2, *yfwd, k2tog, k2; rep from
* to last 2 sts, k2.

Row 22: Purl.

Work from chart for 4 rows.

INCREASE FOR THUMB

Keeping patt correct:

Row 27: Work 23 sts from chart, inc 1, work 2, inc 1, pattern to end (52 sts).

Row 28: Work 25 sts from chart, p2 using B and D only, work 25 sts to end. Use separate wrappings of yarns A and C for right and left sides. Thumb sts are knitted in yarns B and D only throughout.

Row 29: Work 25 sts, inc 1, k4, inc 1, work 25 sts (54 sts).

Keeping patt correct, work from chart increasing for thumb gusset as set in previous rows until 62 sts.

Next row (Row 16 of chart): Work 25 sts from chart, work 12 sts of thumb gusset, turn.

Work on 12 sts only.

Next row: Purl.

Work a further 10 rows in St st, or until required length, ending in a purl row.

Next row: K1, *k2tog; rep from * to last st, k1.

Break off yarn leaving approx. 15–20cm (6–8in), thread through sts and draw together. Secure yarn and sew sides together.

Rejoin yarn, pick up 2 sts at base of thumb and complete Row 16 of chart.

Next row: Keeping patt correct work, 24 sts, [p2tog] twice, work to end (50 sts).

Complete chart.

Work 6 rows in St st using yarns A and C only.

SHAPE TOP

Next row: K1, sl1, k1, psso, k20, k2tog, sl1, k1, psso, k20, k2tog, k1 (46 sts).

Work 3 rows St st.

Next row: K1, sl1, k1, psso, k18, k2tog, sl1, k1, psso, k18, k2tog, k1 (42 sts).

Work 3 rows St st.

Next row: K1, sl1, k1, psso, k16, k2tog, sl1, k1, psso, k16, k2tog, k1 (38 sts).

Next row: Purl.

Next row: K1, sl1, k1, psso, k16, k2tog, sl1, k1, psso, k16, k2tog, k1 (34 sts).

Next row: Purl.

Next row: K1, sl1, k1, psso, k14, k2tog, sl1, k1, psso, k14, k2tog, k1 (30 sts).

Break off yarn.

FINISHING

Sew in all loose ends, block and press fabric. Sew up side seams using mattress stitch, taking care to match up pattern. Make twisted cord and thread through eyelets.

FIRE-STARTER

Try exchanging the twisted cord for a silk ribbon or similar material to add a touch of elegance to the design.

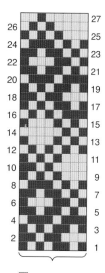

☐ A and C
■ B and D

Cabled Muff

Enjoy your muff through all the seasons! It is designed to be worn with cuffs outside, but for extra warmth, tuck them inside for a double thickness. The built-in storage pocket is handy for small items. Designed by Kimberly Cherubin.

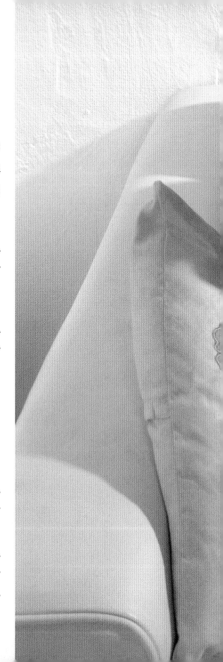

YARN

Rowan *Cashsoft Aran* (57% merino, 33% microfibre, 10% cashmere), approx 50g/87m per ball

2 balls of Oatmeal 01

NEEDLES

Four 4.50mm (US 7) double-pointed needles (dpns) or two 4.50mm (US 7) circular needles
Set of 4.00mm (US 6) double pointed needles (dpns) or two 4.00mm (US 6) circular needles
One cable needle
One crochet hook

BUTTON

Decorative button or toggle

TENSION

16 sts and 28 rows = 10cm (4in) square measured over St st using four 4.50mm (US 7) dpns and two 4.00mm (US 6) circular needles

TO FIT

One size

SKILL LEVEL

Intermediate

SPECIAL ABBREVIATIONS

See page 95 for information on: m1f, C6B.

MUFF

Using 4.00mm (US 6) needles and two strands of yarn, CO 36 sts, join. If using two circular needles, CO using long-tail method.

Rows 1–24: K2, p2 to end.

INC ROWS

If desired, switch to 4.50mm (US 7) needles.

Row 25: *P6, m1f; rep from * four times, p6 (41 sts).

Row 26: Purl.

Row 27: *P7, m1f; rep from * four times, p6 (46 sts).

Row 28: Purl.

Row 29: *P8, m1f; rep from * four times, p6 (51 sts).

Row 30: Purl.

Row 31: *P9, m1f; rep from * five times, p6 (56 sts).

Row 32: Purl.

START CABLE PATTERN

Round 33: K1, p1, k1, p1, *k2, p2, k6, p2, k2, p1, k1, p1; rep from * twice, k1.

Round 34: K2, p1, k1, *k2, p2, k6, p2, k3, p1, k1; rep from * twice, k1.

Round 35: K1, p1, k1, p1, *k2, p2, k6, p2, k2, p1, k1, p1; rep from * twice, k1.

Round 36: K2, p1, k1, *k2, p2, k6, p2, k3, p1, k1; rep from * twice, k1.

Round 37: K1, p1, k1, p1, *k2, p2, k6, p2, k2, p1, k1, p1; rep from * twice, k1.

Round 38: K2, p1, k1, k2, p2, C6B, p2, k3, p1, k1; rep from * twice, k1.

Rounds 39–50: Rep Rounds 33–38 twice more.

POCKET HOLE

Rows 51–62: Cont in cable pattern as set in Rows 33–50 but DO NOT join at end of row. At the end of this and foll rows, turn work and continue in pattern on WS as follows:

Rows 52 (54, 56, 58, 60, 62): K2, p1, k1, p2, k2, p6, k2, p2, k1, p1, k1; rep from * twice, p1.

NOTE: Knit first and last sts for all rows for a clean edge on pocket hole. Cont in rounds.

Rounds 63–80: Rep Rounds 33–38 three times.

START DECREASE

Round 81: Purl.

Round 82: *P9, p2tog; rep from * four times, p1 (51 sts).

Rnd 83: Purl.

Row 84: *P8, p2tog; rep from * four times, p1 (46 sts).

Round 85: Purl.

Row 86: *P7, p2tog; rep from * four times, p1 (41 sts).

Round 87: Purl.

Round 88: *P6, p2tog; rep from * four times, p1 (36 sts).

Rounds 89–112: K2, p2 to end. Cast off.

Break off yarn, weave in ends.

FINISHING

Make pocket by working in cast-off sts for pocket hole in Muff body, pick up and knit through back (or inner) loop around hole. Work in St st such that knit sides face each other on the inside of the pocket. Knit to desired depth of pocket – 7.5–10cm (3–4in). Cast off using two-needle method. Sew a decorative button to either side of the centre of the pocket hole. Using crochet hook, join one strand of yarn on opposite side of pocket hole, where you attached the button. Chain sts to a length of about 2.5cm (1in) (long enough to go over a button) and tie end. Join yarn to create button loop.

ZIP IT GOOD!

Use yarns in different colours for cuffs and body, or work in stripes. If you are handy with a needle, you can choose to zip the pocket closed instead of using a button and hook; simply sew a short zip to the inside of the pocket.

Knitting

TENSION (GAUGE) AND SELECTING CORRECT NEEDLE SIZE

Tension (gauge) can differ quite dramatically between knitters. This is because of the way that the needles and the yarn are held. So if your tension (gauge) does not match that stated in the pattern, you should change your needle size following this simple rule:

- If your knitting is too loose, your tension (gauge) will read that you have fewer stitches and rows than the given tension (gauge), and you will need to change to a smaller needle to make the stitch size smaller.
- If your knitting is too tight, your tension (gauge) will read that you have more stitches and rows than the given tension (gauge), and you will need to change to a thicker needle to make the stitch size bigger.

Please note that if the projects in this book are not knitted to the correct tension (gauge), yarn quantities will be affected.

KNITTING A TENSION SWATCH

No matter how excited you are about a new knitting project, take the time to knit a tension swatch for accurate sizing. Use the same needles, yarn and stitch pattern as those that will be used for the main work and knit a sample at least 12.5cm (5in) square. Smooth out the finished piece on a flat surface, but do not stretch it.

To check the stitch tension, place a ruler horizontally on the sample, measure 10cm (4in) across and mark with a pin at each end. Count the number of stitches between the pins. To check the row tension, place a ruler vertically on the sample, measure 10cm (4in) and mark with pins. Count the number of rows between the pins. If the number of stitches and rows is greater than specified in the pattern, make a new swatch using larger needles; if it is less, make a new swatch using smaller needles.

MAKING A SLIP KNOT

A slip knot is the basis of all casting-on techniques and is therefore the starting point for almost everything you do in knitting and crochet.

1
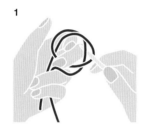
1 Wind the yarn around two fingers twice as shown. Insert a knitting needle through the first (front) strand and under the second (back) one.

2

2 Using the needle, pull the back strand through the front one to form a loop.

3

3 Holding the loose ends of the yarn with your left hand, pull the needle upwards, thus tightening the knot. Pull the ball end of the yarn again to tighten the knot further.

CASTING ON

'Casting on' is the term used for making a row of stitches to be used as a foundation for your knitting.

1

1 Make a slip knot 100cm (40in) from the end of the yarn. Hold the needle in your right hand with the ball end of the yarn over your index finger. *Wind the loose end of the yarn around your left thumb from front to back.

2

2 Insert the point of the needle under the first strand of yarn on your thumb.

3 With your right index finger, take the ball end of the yarn over the point of the needle.

3

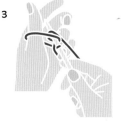

4 Pull a loop through to form the first stitch. Remove your left thumb from the yarn. Pull the loose end to secure the stitch. Repeat from * until the required number of stitches have been cast on.

4

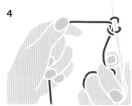

THE BASIC STITCHES

Knit and purl stitches form the basis of all knitted fabrics. The knit stitch is the easiest to learn and once you have mastered this you can move on to the purl stitch, which is the reverse of the knit stitch.

KNIT STITCH

1

1 Hold the needle with the cast-on stitches in your left hand, with the loose yarn at the back of the work. Insert the right-hand needle from left to right through the front of the first stitch on the left-hand needle.

2

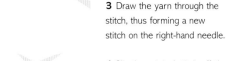

2 Wrap the yarn from left to right over the point of the right-hand needle.

3 Draw the yarn through the stitch, thus forming a new stitch on the right-hand needle.

3

4 Slip the original stitch off the left-hand needle, keeping the new stitch on the right-hand needle.

5 To knit a row, repeat steps 1 to 4 until all the stitches have been transferred from the left-hand needle to the right-hand needle. Turn the work, transferring the needle with the stitches to your left hand to work the next row.

4

PURL STITCH

1

2

3

4

1 Hold the needle with the stitches in your left hand, with the loose yarn at the front of the work. Insert the right-hand needle from right to left into the front of the first stitch on the left-hand needle.

2 Wrap the yarn from right to left, up and over the point of the right-hand needle.

3 Draw the yarn through the stitch, thus forming a new stitch on the right-hand needle.

4 Slip the original stitch off the left-hand needle, keeping the new stitch on the right-hand needle.

5 To purl a row, repeat steps 1 to 4 until all the stitches have been transferred from the left-hand needle to the right-hand needle. Turn the work, transferring the needle with the stitches to your left hand to work the next row.

INCREASING AND DECREASING

Many projects will require some shaping, either just to add interest or to make them fit comfortably. Shaping is achieved by increasing or decreasing the number of stitches you are working.

INCREASING

The simplest method of increasing one stitch is to work into the front and back of the same stitch.

On a knit row, knit into the front of the stitch to be increased, then before slipping it off the needle, place the right-hand needle behind the left-hand one and knit again into the back of it (inc). Slip the original stitch off the left-hand needle. On a purl row, purl into the front of the stitch to be increased, then before slipping it off the needle, purl again into the back of it. Slip the original stitch off the left-hand needle.

DECREASING

The simplest method of decreasing one stitch is to work two stitches together.

On a knit row, insert the right-hand needle from left to right through two stitches instead of one, then knit them together as one stitch. This is called knit two together (k2tog).

On a purl row, insert the right-hand needle from right to left through two stitches instead of one, then purl them together as one stitch. This is called purl two together (p2tog).

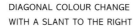

INTARSIA STITCHES

'Intarsia' is where the pattern is worked in large blocks of colour at a time, requiring a separate ball of yarn for each area of colour.

DIAGONAL COLOUR CHANGE WITH A SLANT TO THE LEFT

DIAGONAL COLOUR CHANGE WITH A SLANT TO THE RIGHT

VERTICAL COLOUR CHANGE

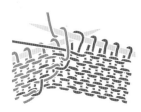

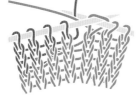

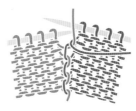

On a wrong-side row, with the yarns at the front of the work, take the first colour over the second colour, drop it, then pick up the second colour underneath the first colour, thus crossing the two colours together.

On a right-side row, with the yarns at the back of the work, take the first colour over the second colour, drop it, then pick up the second colour underneath the first colour, thus crossing the two colours.

Work in the first colour to the colour change, then drop the first colour, pick up the second colour underneath the first colour, crossing the two colours over before working the next stitch in the second colour. After a colour change, work the first stitch firmly to prevent a gap forming between colours.

FAIR ISLE STITCHES

Yarn that is not in use is left at the back of the work until needed. The loops formed by this are called 'floats' and it is important that they are not pulled too tightly when working the next stitch, as this will pull your knitting.

  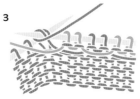 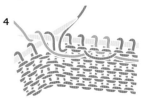

1 On a knit row, hold the first colour in your right hand and the second colour in your left hand. Knit the required number of stitches as usual with the first colour, carrying the second colour loosely across the wrong side of the work.

2 To knit a stitch in the second colour, insert the right-hand needle into the next stitch, then draw a loop through from the yarn held in the left hand, carrying the yarn in the right hand loosely across the wrong side until required.

3 On a purl row, hold the yarns as for the knit rows. Purl the required number of stitches as usual with the first colour, carrying the second colour loosely across these stitches on the wrong side of the work.

4 To purl a stitch in the second colour, insert the right-hand needle into the next stitch, then draw a loop through from the yarn held in the left hand, carrying the yarn in the right hand loosely across the wrong side until next required.

- -

CASTING OFF

This is the most commonly used method of securing stitches at the end of a piece of knitting. The cast-off edge should have the same 'give' or elasticity as the fabric; cast off in the stitch used for the main fabric unless the pattern directs otherwise.

KNITWISE

Knit two stitches. *Using the point of the left-hand needle, lift the first stitch on the right-hand needle over the second, then drop it off the needle. Knit the next stitch and repeat from * until all stitches have been worked off the left-hand needle and only one stitch remains on the right-hand needle. Cut the yarn, leaving enough to sew in the end. Thread the end through the stitch, then slip it off the needle. Draw the yarn up firmly to fasten off.

PURLWISE

Purl two stitches. *Using the point of the left-hand needle, lift the first stitch on the right-hand needle over the second and drop it off the needle. Purl the next stitch and repeat from * until all the stitches have been worked off the left-hand needle and only one stitch remains on the right-hand needle. Cut the yarn, leaving enough to sew in the end. Thread the end through the stitch, then slip it off the needle. Draw the yarn up firmly to fasten off.

Crochet

TENSION

This is the number of rows and stitches per centimetre or inch, usually measured over a 10cm (4in) square. The tension will determine the size of the finished item. The correct tension is given at the beginning of each pattern. Crochet a small swatch, using the recommended yarn and hook, to make sure you are working to the correct tension. If your work is too loose, choose a hook that is one size smaller, and if it is too tight, choose a hook the next size up. When making clothes, it is important to check tension before you start; it is not worth making something the wrong size. When measuring work, lay it on a flat surface and always measure at the centre, rather than at the side edges.

BASIC STITCHES

Start by making a series of chains – around 10 will be enough. Now you're ready to practise the following stitches.

SLIP STITCH (SS)

1 This is the shortest stitch and mostly used for joining and shaping. Insert the hook into a stitch or chain (always remember to insert the hook under both strands of the stitch), yarn over the hook from the back to the front of the hook, and draw the hook through the stitch and the loop on the hook. You are left with just 1 loop on the hook. This is 1 slip stitch.

DOUBLE CROCHET (DC)

1 Insert the hook into the second chain from the hook, yarn over the hook, draw the loop through your work.

2 Yarn over and draw the hook through both loops on the hook; 1 loop on the hook. This is 1 double crochet.

3 Repeat into the next stitch or chain until you've reached the end of the row, make 1 chain stitch – this is your turning chain – turn the work and work 1 double crochet into each stitch of the previous row, ensuring that you insert the hook under both loops of the stitch you are crocheting into.

HALF TREBLE CROCHET (HTR)

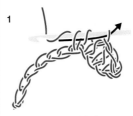

1 Yarn over the hook before inserting the hook into the third chain from the hook, yarn over, draw 1 loop through the work, yarn over, draw through all 3 loops on the hook; 1 loop on the hook. This is 1 half treble crochet.

2 When you reach the end of the row, make 2 chains – this counts as the first stitch of the next row. Turn the work, skip the first half treble crochet of the previous row and insert the hook into the second stitch of the new row. Continue to work until the end of the row. At the end of the row, work the last half treble into the top of the turning chain of the row below.

TREBLE CROCHET (TR)

1 Start by wrapping the yarn over the hook and insert the hook into the fourth chain from the hook, yarn over, draw 1 loop through the work

2 Yarn over, draw through the first 2 loops on the hook, yarn over, draw through the remaining 2 loops on the hook; 1 loop on the hook. This is 1 treble crochet.

3 When you reach the end of the row, make 3 chains. These count as the first stitch of the next row. Turn the work and skip the first treble crochet of the previous row; insert the hook into the second stitch of the new row. Continue to work until the end of the row, inserting the last treble crochet into the top of the turning chain of the row below.

1

2

BASIC TECHNIQUES

As well as working from right to left in rows, crochet can also be worked in a circular fashion (referred to as working in the round), or even in a continuous spiral to make seamless items such as hats, bags and other rounded objects.

MAKING FABRIC – WORKING IN ROWS

1

2

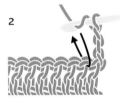

3

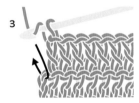

1 Make as many chain stitches as you require. This row is called the base chain. Insert the hook into the second chain from the hook (not counting the chain on the hook) for double crochet, third chain from the hook for treble crochet.

2 Work from right to left, inserting the hook under two of the three threads in each chain.

3 When you reach the end of the row, work one or more turning chains, depending on the height of the stitch.

Turning chains should be worked as follows:
Double crochet: 1 chain.
Half treble: 2 chains.
Treble: 3 chains.
Double treble: 4 chains.
Triple treble: 5 chains.

Now turn the work to begin working on the next row (remember always to turn your work in the same direction). When working in double crochet, insert the hook into the first stitch in the new row and work each stitch to the end of the row, excluding the turning chain. For all other stitches, unless the pattern states otherwise, the turning chain counts as the first stitch. Skip 1 stitch and work each stitch to the end of the row, including the top of the turning chain.

MAKING FABRIC – WORKING IN THE ROUND

1 **2**

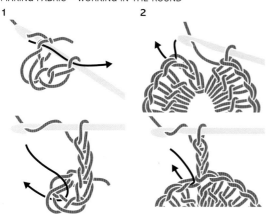

1 Crochet in the round starts with a ring. To make a ring, make a series of chains and join the last chain to the first with a slip stitch.

2 To make the first round, work a starting chain to the height of the stitch you are working in. Then work as many stitches as you need into the centre of the ring and finish the round with a slip stitch into the first stitch.

3 Begin the second and subsequent rounds with a starting chain (worked the same way as a turning chain, with the number of chains depending on the stitch you are working: see page 92). Then insert the hook under the top 2 loops of each stitch in the previous round. At the end of the round, join to the top of the starting chain with a slip stitch, as in step 2.

INCREASING

As with knitting, fabric is often shaped by increasing the number of stitches in a row or round. To increase, simply work an additional stitch into the next stitch. A single increase is made by working 2 stitches into the same stitch. You can of course increase by more than 1 stitch at a time.

DECREASING

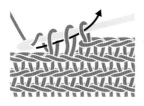

DC2TOG
To decrease 1 stitch in double crochet (dc2tog), insert hook into the next stitch, yarn over, draw through the work, insert hook into the next stitch, yarn over, draw through the work, yarn over, draw through all 3 loops, leaving just 1 loop on the hook.

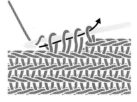

SC3TOG
To decrease by 2 stitches in double crochet, work 3 stitches together (dc3tog) by working as for dc2tog until you have 3 loops on the hook. Insert the hook into the next stitch, yarn over, draw through the work, yarn over and draw through all 4 loops.

TR2TOG
To decrease 1 stitch in treble crochet (tr2tog), yarn over, insert hook into next stitch, yarn over, draw through work, yarn over, draw through 2 loops, yarn over, insert hook into next stitch, yarn over, draw through work, yarn over, draw through 2 loops, yarn over, draw through all 3 loops.

FINISHING OFF

There are various ways of sewing up seams.

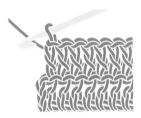

FASTENING OFF

Cut the yarn, leaving roughly 13cm (5in). Make 1 chain and draw the tail through the chain and pull firmly. Weave the end a few centimetres or an inch in one direction and then back the other way for a neat and secure finish.

FLAT STITCH

This seam creates an almost invisible join. Lay the two sections right-side up, with the stitches aligned. Using a tapestry needle, insert under the lower half of the edge stitch on one section, then under the upper half of the edge stitch on the opposite section.

Abbreviations

KNITTING ABBREVIATIONS

alt = alternate/alternating
beg = beginning
cn = cable needle
CO = cast on
cont = continue
dec = decrease
dpn = double-pointed needle
foll = following
inc = increase/increasing
k = knit
k2tog = knit two together
LH = left-hand
M = marker
m1 = make one st. Lift the horizontal strand between the st just worked and next st, then knit through back of this thread.
MC = main colour
p = purl
p2tog = purl two together
patt = pattern
PM = place marker
prev = previous
psso = pass slipped stitch over
rem = remaining
rep = repeat
RH = right-hand
rnd = round
RS = right side
sep = separate
sl = slip
SM = slip marker

skpo = slip 1 st knitwise, knit 1 st, pass slipped stitch over
sppo = slip 1 st purlwise, purl 1 st, pass slipped stitch over
ssk = slip 1 st, slip 1 st, knit the next st
St st = stocking stitch
st(s) = stitch(es)
tog = together
TS = thumb section
tbl = through back of loops
WS = wrong side
yfwd = yarn forward
yo = yarn over needle
yrn = yarn around needle

CROCHET ABBREVIATIONS

ch = chain
dc = double crochet
ss = slip stitch
tch = turning chain
yrh = yarn around hook

SPECIAL ABBREVIATIONS SPOT-ON MITTENS

Double cast off = Hold two LH knitting needles together with RS of work facing each other. With a third needle, knit first st on front and back needles together. Knit next st on front and back needles together and cast off as normal by bringing loop of first st over second.

SPECIAL ABBREVIATIONS TEXTURED GLOVES

MB = Make bobble; [k1, yo, k1, yo, k1] into 1 st, turn, p5, turn, k5, turn, p2tog, k1, p2tog tbl, turn, k3tog.

SPECIAL ABBREVIATIONS STRIPED MITTENS

inc 1 = Increase 1 st by knitting into front and back of next st.
m1l and m1r (see Special Abbreviations Bow Belles Mittens).

SPECIAL ABBREVIATIONS LACE GLOVES

BS = Bead stitch.
inc 1 = Increase 1 st by knitting into front and back of next st.
sl1 = Slip 1 st knitwise.
yfwd = Yarn forward under the needle (as if for purl st).

SPECIAL ABBREVIATIONS FAIR ISLE WARMERS

C2F = Slip 1 st on to dpn and hold at back, knit 1 st from the left needle, knit st from dpn.

SPECIAL ABBREVIATIONS FLIP-TOP MITTS

trtog = Treble together.

SPECIAL ABBREVIATIONS CABLE MITTENS

FC = Front cross; sl 2 sts to double-pointed needle and hold in front, p1, then k2 from dpn.
BC = Back cross; Sl 1 st to dpn and hold in back, k2, then p1 from dpn.
MK = Make knot; [k1, p1, k1, p1, k1, p1, k1] in 1 st, making 7 sts from one; then with point of LH needle pass the second, third, fourth, fifth, sixth and seventh stitches on the RH needle sep over the last st made, completing the knot.
CP = Bobbly cable pattern.

SPECIAL ABBREVIATIONS BOW BELLES MITTENS

m1l = Make 1 stitch slanting to the left; insert the left needle from front to back into the bar between the needles. With the right needle, knit through the back.
m1r = Make 1 stitch slanting to the right; insert the left needle from back to front into the bar between the needles. With the right needle, knit through the front.

SPECIAL ABBREVIATIONS PEACOCK FLIP MITTENS

C2F = Slip 1 st on to dpn and hold at back, knit 1 st from the left needle, knit st from dpn.

SPECIAL ABBREVIATIONS CABLED MUFF

m1f = From the front, lift loop between stitches with left needle, knit into back of loop.
C6B = Slip first 3 sts knitwise on to cable needle and hold at back of work, k3, then knit the slipped sts (while they are still on the cable needle).

KITCHENER STITCH

With the stitches on two parallel, double-pointed needles, make sure that the working yarn is coming from the back needle. Take the tapestry needle through the first stitch on the front needle as if to purl and leave the stitch on the needle. Next, go through the first stitch on the back needle as if to knit – leave this stitch on the needle. Keeping the working yarn below the needles, work 2 sts on the front needle, followed by 2 sts on the back needle across the row as follows:
On front needle, go through the first st as if to knit and drop it off the needle. Go through the second st as if to knit and leave it on the needle. Tighten the yarn. On the back needle, go through the first st as if to purl and drop it off the needle. Go through second st as if to knit and leave it on the needle. Tighten the yarn. When there is only one stitch on one needle, go through the front stitch as if to drop it off the needle. Go through the back stitch as if to purl and drop it off the needle. Pull the tail to the inside and weave in.

Resources

Debbie Bliss Yarns
c/o Designer Yarns Ltd.
Unit 8-10 Newbridge Industrial Estate
Pitt Street
Keighley
West Yorkshire
BD21 4PQ
01535 664222
www.designeryarns.uk.com

Jamieson & Smith Ltd
90 North Road
Lerwick
Shetland Islands
ZE1 0PQ
01595 693579
www.jamiesonandsmith.co.uk

Lana Gross UK
2 Riverside
Milngavie
Glasgow
G62 6PL
0141 956 3121
www.lanagrossa.co.uk

Noro Yarns
See Debbie Bliss

Rowan Yarns
Green Lane Mill
Holmfirth HD9 2BR
01484 681881
www.knitrowan.com

Rowan Yarn Classics
Green Lane Mill
Holmfirth HD9 2BR
01484 681881
www.ryclassic.com

Twilley's
c/o Angel Yarns
Angel House
77 North Street
Portslade
East Sussex
BN41 1DZ
0870 766 6212
www.angelyarns.com